Pass the Oxtail

(BEFORE THE WORLD ENDS)

...

An Occasionally-Friendly Discourse on Colossal Randomness and the End of Everything

BY BOWEN CRAIG AND
KELBOURNE "KELLY" CODLING

ATHENS, GEORGIA

PASS THE OXTAIL (BEFORE THE WORLD ENDS):
An Occasionally-Friendly Discourse on Colossal
Randomness and the End of Everything

Copyright © 2023 by Bowen Craig and
Kelbourne "Kelly" Codling

ISBN: 979-8-9867043-4-0
Printed in the United States of America

Published in the United States of America by
Bilbo Books Publishing in Athens, Georgia.
www.BilboBooks.com
bilbobookspublishing@gmail.com
(706) 549-1597

COVER PHOTO: MARIGOLD SOLUTIONS
MARIGOLDSOLUTIONS.CO

COVER AND INTERIOR DESIGN: LUCKY DOG PRESS, LLC

BACKGROUND

Kelly and I are friends by this point, having long since worked together on his earlier book, his biography/autobiography/cookbook/ Jamaican-patois-to-American-English dictionary/anecdote treasure trove called *True Believer* (Buy it, it's good, and I'm not in the least bit biased.). In the process of working on *True Believer*, Kelly and I wound up getting to know each other well and discovered that we're both natural amateur philosophers. We both just sort of philosophize for fun all the time anyway, so we thought it would be both fun and interesting to co-write a philosophy book…and a good excuse to hang out together and cross-philosophize. OK, I'll admit it, I wanted to figure out a way to legally write "hanging out with Kelly Codling" off my taxes. And damn it, that's what I did. So, this is Bowen Craig's and Kelbourne "Kelly" Codling's book of philosophy. Enjoy.

— Bowen Craig

INTRODUCTION PART I
Kelbourne "Kelly" Coburn

I trust in God. He is my advisor and counselor. That's why I named my first book *True Believer*.

Here's my story of how this second book came into being. I was talking to some of my customers about my first book, and new ideas started to come my way. I credit God with the ideas. They're not mine. They're His.

So, I got with Bowen, my publisher and co-author, and we brainstormed about writing about things that made me happy in the past, things that make me happy (and/or angry) in the present and things that make him happy. I don't know what will happen in the future, but it may take three or four books to cover everything.

The first book was mainly about my coming to U.S, and all of the things I've been through that led me to where I am now. This book is going to be more general. I'll try to mention all of the things that I didn't remember when we did the first book. I've tried to add more of my feelings, ideas, and philosophies to this one.

I've gotten a lot of good advice in my life. My mother, my grandmother, my friends, my family, even my customers have all advised me about lots of things. I want to honor them all.

It is so amazing how the mind works – if you use it wisely. The brain and the soul work together. We have to listen to them both very carefully or we end up doing the wrong thing. Most people don't listen, and they end up on the wrong side of the fence. Once you're on the wrong side, it's hard to get yourself back. Listen to yourself. In *True Believer* I wrote, "I've made a habit of listening to that inner voice, that little internal warning system that some call intuition, others call God, and still others call common sense. That little guy has saved my ass numerous times."

That little voice inside of me is what keeps me going, what keeps me sane, what keeps me always on the right side of the fence. When you tell a negative person that you're going to do this thing or that, and they say it's impossible, just laugh. Do not listen to the naysayers. Laugh because they don't know what you're made of, and unless they radically change their outlook on life, they never will.

...

Let me take you back to 1969. The year of Woodstock. The year of the Moon Landing (If that was real. Dum, dum-dum!). Definitely the year that I moved from Jamaica to America, to Washington D.C., a crazy, tumultuous year, a year of anti-war protests, a year of black pride, a year of boundless hope and righteous anger. I could have easily gone the route of stealing, conning, killing, dealing drugs. I had plenty of opportunities. Thanks mainly to my mother, I followed a different path. I went to college, studied business, drove a cab, worked at a hospital morgue, went to more college, and began to learn the strange ways of America. I paid attention at every job I had, learning what worked and what didn't. When I eventually went into business for myself, I put all of those lessons into practice.

Working for myself is one of the most enjoyable things in life. Not only do I love what I do every day, and not have to answer to a boss, but it makes me think on a broader scale. My mind is always open. I try to learn something new every day, and I have so very many teachers: newborn babies, my customers, birds, mammals, trees, flowers, everything, occasionally even Bowen. But, unlike Bowen, the things that cannot talk generally teach more profound lessons than those that can.

INTRODUCTION PART II
Bowen Craig

Why this book? The short answer is that I had so much fun working with Kelly on his first book that I wanted a good excuse to do another one. The long answer is utter bullshit. I could type it here, but it's really long, and total crap. So I'll save the space for more interesting stuff, like Kelly's and my ideas about pretty much everything we care about: the unknown and unseen, spirituality (He calls it religion.), conspiracy theories, politics, common sense, the ways of the animals, life lessons the rest of the world should learn from the Caribbean, uncommon sense, prophets ancient and modern, more politics, government fear tactics and other obvious control mechanisms (re: "Pandemic"), completely not-at-all-common sense, Biblical plagues, protests, Biblical lessons, hope, love, business ethics, Biblical predictions for the End Times, Southern culture, American history, world history, propaganda and its ripple effects, love, music, spicy food, pandemics and their ripple effects, Jamaican farm remedies for pretty much every "disease" that exists, community, and a bunch of other stuff.

At first, we had no idea that, while we were writing, the whole world would go batshit crazy, also known as "Our general, extremely overblown reaction to the novel coronavirus."

I was going to list every topic we covered, but if you've read this far, just go ahead and read the rest of the book. You've already bought (or stolen) it. You might as well enjoy it.

PROLOGUE

The vague plan for this book was for the two of us to sit down for an hour or so every few weeks, talk about whatever we feel like discussing that day, and then I'd write it up. We expected world events to factor into our conversation choices…unless of course the world ended before we finished the book. In that case, Kelly's probably going to heaven, and I hope he sends me a postcard.

We had no idea that the Powers-That-Be would try and convince us the world really was going to end as we were in the process of writing the book.

…

One afternoon between his lunch and dinner rushes, Kelly and I were sitting at his second restaurant, the one nestled cozily between a bunch of Athens' University of Georgia student apartment complexes. Before we could get into anything resembling philosophy, I noticed his vending machines, the ones that, for a mere 25 cents, dispense one of a variety of tiny, highly-breakable, going-to-be-discarded-faster-than-a-goldfish-"won"-at-a-county-fair-throw-a-dart-at-a-balloon-with-the-face-of-a-clown-on-it, little pieces of plastic crap. They generally cost only a quarter and you (presumably to give to your child, but not really since adult men really never grow out of playing with toys, we're just supposed to pretend we do) put in the quarter, turn the metal handle 180 degrees and get a piece of rubber in the shape of the animated star of some Disney movie from 20 years ago. You know exactly what I'm talking about.

It struck me that the very act of getting that toy is fun, much more fun than buying it at a toy store. It's fun, even though you pretty much know you're going to lose it or accidentally swallow it if you're a child, or if you're drunk, or a drunk child. People like the act of turning the handle. People like seeing what they're about to "win," at random. It's a game and people like games. People like carnivals. People are more than willing to overpay for stuff if there's a little gamesmanship involved. This is the entire capitalistic premise behind any business with a Skee Ball machine. Why don't we put stuff other than cheap, plastic toys in those vending machines? Stuff like wedding rings, land deeds, miniature corn cobs, fortunes written in long-dead languages, guesses as to which current Hollywood child actor will be America's 51st president, whatever? Why don't we recognize that fun is fun and add fun to the act of buying other stuff we don't need? What's so wrong with fun? And why do we think we're supposed to stop having fun once we turn nine, or twenty-five, or whatever age when people start routinely telling us to "grow up?" Screw those people.

That's the other premise of this book – FUN.

Philosophy and fun.
Let's see what happens.

TOPIC #1: WEED

Kelly's Jamaican, so I figured we should go ahead and get the part about weed out of the way. You know you were thinking about it.

Ahh, marijuana. This much-maligned, highly loveable, native plant is surrounded on all sides by peoples' opinions about it. It's just a freaking plant, and if you look up the origins of its illegality, the whole thing is about capitalism and racism, probably the two most powerful "isms" of our time.

...

[[[QUICK HISTORICAL INTERLUDE – look up the antecedent to the least winnable war ever, The Drug War – the illegalizing of the harmless, sometimes helpful and medicinal, shockingly-less-addictive-than-alcohol-tobacco-or, God knows, cell phones, plant. Just plant, not drug, just plant. Google "William Randolph Hearst," "hemp production in the early 20th century," "how white people are afraid of black men/jazz music and have been for some time," and "how it's incredibly easy to convince people of something completely insane when you own pretty much every newspaper in the country." And yeah, this is foreshadowing. OK, interlude over.]]]

...

When we started talking about it, Kelly, being a True Believer, began with Biblical citations. I've heard this track of rhapsodizing before, and I'm not putting it down. Maybe Kelly's right. Personally,

I don't need scriptural precedent to know that it's a ridiculous control mechanism for a government to say a plant, any plant, is illegal. Illegal plants? That's patently crazy. But I want to stress that I'm not putting down Kelly's religion. In fact, I'm a bit jealous of how easy he makes faith look.

"It's not a drug. It's a healing plant," Kelly says.

Yeah, I can get behind that.

As I'm typing this, it would seem, from an alien-visiting-Earth-and-just-watching-us-run-around-and-all-be-morons perspective, that we're living in a bit of a slowly-changing country with regard to our national attitude about weed. That's not really true. Most people think it's pretty harmless…BECAUSE IT'S HARMLESS. The difference now, the reason it's finally, ever so slowly, becoming legal is that America's money men have finally realized that they can make a damn fortune off it. Those guys don't care about much of anything, but they do like money. The only reason they haven't jumped headfirst into it (the reason it's taking so long to get legalized nationally) is that those same money men also realize that it's not a pill made from an obscure Amazonian plant. Anyone can grow weed in his basement or his yard, or really anywhere. In other words, they know they can't really control the "means of production" and that's how those greedy bastards think.

Prohibiting anything that isn't generally considered wrong by the majority of a democratic society never works. Read up on Prohibition, those strange years in America when alcohol was illegal. People still drank booze, quite a bit of it. Speakeasies were everywhere. Moonshine stills littered the mountainsides. Moonshiners' running away from Revenuers (the Booze Police) was, believe it or not, the origin of Nascar. Prohibition gave us organized crime, and a template, a failed template, an unbelievably cruel and horrifically-failed template, for the 20th century Drug War – which of course the money men ran with in order to do what they do, make money. The money men own the politicians, and can easily afford to rent a few affable TV and radio bloviators, so their will is far too often our command. Kelly and I will get to governing philosophy later. We're trying not to cross the metaphorical streams too much and will try to limit our rants to one subject per chapter. It probably won't work out like we planned, but that's the idea. Finish the book and you tell us if we succeeded. {Hint – We didn't.}

Personally, I believe that legal moralizing only works when somewhere around 90% of the population thinks that what's being prohibited is actually inherently wrong. We all pretty much agree that murder is wrong, so laws against murder work. We all pretty much agree that rape is bad, so anti-rape laws work. We're a little fuzzier about drugs. These days, those of us who pay any attention whatsoever can tell that the Pharma companies have gamed the Drug War in the evilest possible way. They profit off our misery much like organized crime bosses. And, since their political bribes work wonders, they, like the cartels and Taliban opium farmers, are the winners in the Drug War. Who are the losers? Everybody else.

The Pharma assholes, fear, racism, and booze's stranglehold on the American buzz are the main reason that drugs – and by drugs I mean medicine without the doctors – was ever illegal at all. According to Kelly, "It was always a scam to control us. America used to fly South and crop-dust the islands with plant-killing pesticides."

A quick and mildly-clever way to point out this quicksand of ironic nonsense would be to put into practice my political fantasy of some enterprising, dewy, first-term Congressman (who understands irony) to point out the lunacy of illegalizing plants by proposing a bill to ban tulips. Everybody knows that only those filthy, rapist, lazy, thieving, windmill-crazy Dutch bastards grow tulips. Those lazy, finger-in-the-dike Dutch Euro-fuckers clearly just don't want to work. They just want to tulip around all day in their weird semi-French language. Do we want a country overrun by the tulip-loving Dutch? They'd replace ketchup with mayonnaise. Everyone would be forced to wear wooden shoes. Power would be generated from wind and the sun. Does that sound like freedom to you? Come on, people. Wake up.

Anyway, Kelly and I talked about marijuana on our first day. We both figured that everyone would want us to, and everyone would just kind of assume that Kelly, being Jamaican, would know something profound about weed that the rest of us don't. Sure, that's crazy, since it seems that around 2/3 of this town smokes this particular plant on a regular basis, but people do love their stereotypes. And as stereotypes go, Jamaica's isn't all that bad: Rastafarians, peace, rum, love, really good weed, reggae music, good coffee, hurricanes, more weed, a cool-sounding slang plus-accent combination so unique and deep that, even though it's English you still can't understand what Jamaicans are saying but you nevertheless think how they're saying it is awesome, ox-tail, sailboats, Bob Marley, even more weed, bright multi-colored hats which allow wearers to put off showering for a few more days, guava, jerk chicken, and a little more weed.

That's pretty much the world's stereotype about Jamaica. It's like Greenland. Nobody hates the place, it's an interesting destination for anyone around the world, but you don't need to have a working knowledge of sled dogs to travel in January. America's stereotype is more schizophrenic: people want to visit America, people respect American military might, people hate American military might, people think we just go around shooting each other like it's still the Old West (because in some of our minds, it still is), overcrowded prisons, racism, money, beautiful and scantily-clad women, the possibility for social advancement, more money, cowboy hats, horses on lone prairies, unnecessarily expensive healthcare, some more money, really good amusement parks, lawyers run amok, money, cops in mirrored sunglasses, muscle cars, fear, money, crime, guns and more money. It's a mixed bag…but that's what makes it fun.

Get ready America, fully-legal weed is coming soon. It'll be more expensive, but at least our teenagers won't get arrested for carrying around a bag of native plant parts, so that's progress.

TOPIC #2: BELIEF

"I don't go to church, but I read the Bible a lot."

Kelly is one of those religious guys who actually knows waaaaayyyyy more about the Bible than 99% of regular churchgoers. I've found that agnostics and atheists tend to have read more of the Bible than the people who profess to hang their belief systems on that particular book. Kelly is definitely, assuredly, proudly and loudly NEI-THER agnostic nor atheist. He's a believer. The difference between Kelly and the regular churchgoers is that Kelly actually listens to the teachings of Jesus Christ and tries to emulate them when possible.

Compared to Kelly, the regular churchgoers are mainly hypocriti-cal fear-mongers, justifying their own internal horribleosity by twisting the message of the prophet whom they say they worship into whatever suits themselves at the moment. And preachers aren't the bosses of churches. They're the hired help. They're Ronald McDonald, not Ray Kroc. The guys who are powerful from Monday through Saturday don't rest on their seventh day. They make sure their "religious" "lead-ers" conveniently skip the part about Jesus' hating rich people and the it-was-once-basically-a-blood-cult stuff. For lack of a better descriptor, Jesus was a communist, and the idea of sharing scares the living shit out of the money men, then and now. If you couldn't tell, I do not like those hypocritical, faux religious, greedy, hateful shit-fuckers. They're so unKelly…not that I have a strong opinion on the matter.

The Bible is a good book. I'm just not sure it's THE good book, but Kelly disagrees. He's so much of a believer that he titled his/our first book *True Believer*. The other, secondary, meaning to that title choice was that Kelly wanted to encourage readers to believe in themselves, but on the surface the book is about his belief in God.

"I've seen people live. I've seen people die." Kelly's about to launch into an "easier for a camel to fit through the eye of a needle than for a rich man to enter the kingdom of heaven" rant. Here he goes:

"I've seen a lot of hearses. But I've never seen a hearse dragging a U-Haul behind it." His saying was more interesting and visual than most, and far more poetic and tame then my earlier rant, but I was right about the meaning. Money doesn't really mean much. This thing, this universally agreed-upon idea (money), is just that, an idea. It has no inherent value. *You can't eat money.* Well, you *could*, but it'd be terrible. *You can't wear money.* Again, you *could*, but it'd be really uncomfortable and you'd look like a moron. *You can't live in a house made of money.* Well, you *could*, but it wouldn't be any sturdier than building material choices made by two of the Three Little Pigs.

I'm not putting down God. Although I'm less evangelistic about it than Kelly, I do believe there's some sort of higher power. Things fit together far too well for there not to have been a plan behind it all. I just have a hard time reconciling people's opinions about what God is with what it seems to me an all-powerful, omniscient, omnipresent deity would be like. For example, why would something that powerful waste a millisecond worrying about what we think or say about It? I just can't conceive of a deity who's so petty as to care about stuff that small. And when you get into the stupid minutia it seems even sillier. God hating gay marriage? Really? Why? Why do people think an all-powerful deity would ever gives two holy shits about who anyone would marry, or about marriage, or about our social lives, at all? Do you care what fire ants do in their spare time?

I also have a hard time with the idea of God having a gender. Those guys who insist that God is a man always seem like relics from the Middle Ages, but those feminists who insist that God is a woman are equally annoying and just as stubborn and wrong. If God were a man, then there would be a lot more random sex with strangers in Taco Bell bathrooms and the word "alimony" wouldn't exist. If God were a woman would She really have made men like this? If that doesn't convince you, think about it like this. If God is a man that means the God has a penis, and since He's God, it's probably really big. Now keep thinking about that. Picture the Lord's giant phallus. Are you now fantasizing about God? Does the Christian God want you to sexually fantasize about Him? OK, if that doesn't work, try this. If God is a man and has a giant, holy pecker, and if we're made in God's image, doesn't that mean that God has sex or at least thinks about it every seven seconds? Feels a little pagan, doesn't it? Zeus used to straight up rape anyone he wanted. Half the time he'd turn into a bull or a swan and then get to rapin'. But the Greeks didn't think Zeus was the same kind of entity as the Christian (and Jewish and Muslim) God. To them Zeus was closer to a really bad-ass magical warlord. You want to appease the warlord. You want to keep the warlord from paying too much attention to you. But you curse the warlord under your breath a lot because the warlord is not making your life better.

The one notion of God I can totally get behind, however, is the John 4:16 oft-quoted, "God is love." Most of the rest of it seems silly to me. Kelly disagrees.

TOPIC #3: SPIRITUAL GEOMETRY

OK, I'll just go ahead and admit that I don't know much about this idea, but when people talk about it I: A) Recognize that it sounds so plausible, and actually explains a number of ancient mysteries; and B) I wonder why it's not more mainstream.

This is a common theory/observation among fringe anthropologists, New Agers, and really anyone who can think outside of the ludicrously narrow parameters provided by the authors of the "Official Story." I'm talking about the idea of the Egyptian pyramids being antennae, about their possibly having been built by aliens, maybe as spacecraft landing sites, about pre-Christian monuments being aligned according to natural astronomical patterns (Most people do agree on the last one, but not the first two.), about lay lines, about vortexes, about our world having natural patterns that govern our lives without our ever even knowing it. Stonehenge is the most famous pagan monument in the Western world, but there are plenty of others. They're just farther away from London.

I've heard the term "Spiritual Geometry" used to describe some of these ancient mysteries. The precise orientation of ancient monuments shows us just how much more in tune with the natural world those ancient guys (whom we, of course, pity as lovable but clueless morons) were than we are. Kelly believes in the wisdom of ancient peoples, too. He admits that we moderns don't know everything, and older peoples may have known a lot more than we give them credit for.

Our pro-modern bias is always around. We look back on the past, any time, any place, as stupid and, to at least some degree, *quaint.* Adorably stupid, but still stupid. "Those silly fools and their pantheon of gods, their animal sacrifices, and their giant monuments that no one since has ever come close to matching in terms of glory and majesty. Those guys were so stupid, so ill-informed, so primitive. They'd never even *heard* of cell phones."

Watch commercials and notice that it's an advertising trope, a repeating underlying idea in at least 5% of ads, this notion of modern superiority. I'm not crediting ad men with making this idea up. It was already out there, and most people already believed it. The ad guys just routinely tap into it, in part because they're quite lazy.

Humanity hasn't come close to building anything as amazing as the pyramids, the ziggurats, the Hanging Gardens of Babylon, the Colossus at Rhodes, the Library of Alexandria, its nearby Lighthouse (Pharos, at Alexandria) or any of the other, less-celebrated Wonders of the Ancient World, since. Not even close. (Yes, I do know which seven were "labeled" as Wonders, but the others are pretty wondrous, too.) What modern Wonders would even be in the running? Metropolitan Skyscrapers? High-speed trains? Those serenity-robbing, privacy-devouring, soul-crushing beeping nonsense devices that fit in our pockets? Penicillin is pretty good. So is pizza. But does thin-crust, sausage-laden circular cheese and tomato pie really compare with The Sphinx?

One common retort many pro-moderns cite to justify modernity's superiority is technology, usually encapsulated by computers, specifically cell phones. Since Kelly and I are about the only non-cell-phone owners left on the planet, we both find comfort in the fact that we're not *completely* alone in our shared opinion – almost, but not totally. I've heard rumors of a few Buddhist monks and a few screaming, diaper-pooping toddlers who also don't own cell phones, though I can neither confirm nor deny this rumor.

Since we're literally two of the only people either of us knows who haven't bought into that addictive-money-and-time-and-privacy-sucking nonsense, Kelly and I often have wildly self-congratulatory conversations on this topic, and one aspect of it is the inevitable conversations we've had with other people, many other people, *the cell phone people*, who have repeatedly tried to talk us into buying one. According to Kelly, "The conversation always goes something like this. They mention something about a cell phone or ask me to look something up. I tell them I don't own a cell phone, and they're amazed. They say something like, 'Oh, you don't own a cell phone? You're so far behind the times.' I come back with, 'No, I'm clearly a lot farther advanced than you.' They laugh. I never convince them, but I try."

I've had hundreds of similar exchanges in my recent past, too, no exaggeration. I'm even including a comic essay/blog I wrote about this topic in this very book. I think I'll put it right after this chapter, because unlike all of you cell phone addicts, I don't let technology tell ME what to do. Technology is nothing but a tool, a tool to be used BY us, not a burning bush telling us what to do. You think *I'm* quaint? You think I'm *exaggerating* the bit about addiction? Try going just one day without looking at your annoying little beeping pocket rectangle. If you make it one whole entire day, good for you. That's a great start. Now try two days. Then three. Then call me (on a land line) and you can join The Luddite Club. Kelly and I would be happy to have you join us in enlightenment. Club meetings are getting a little lonely with just the two of us.

Kelly and I are not in total agreement about the legacy of Steve Jobs (a rare area of disagreement between us). He thinks Jobs created something amazing, and we just messed it up. I think Jobs created the world's scariest addiction to date. Kelly's also more awestruck by the business sense it took for the super-successful to make themselves who they are or were. Neither of us owns, nor will ever own, Jobs' crowning achievement, the cell phone. And, despite my constant ranting and what I think are some solid logical points, I've gotten absolutely, totally *no one*, zero, zip, null set, zilch, nada, no people, to agree with my premise that cell phones are not only unnecessary but make life measurably worse. But I didn't even have to convince Kelly. He already saw what I see. Those things are stupid.

Back to spiritual geometry, which was supposed to be the theme of this chapter before we meandered away from it. Near the city of Elberton, Georgia, there is/was a large, interesting, pilgrimage-worthy granite monument called The Georgia Guidestones. Though, like Stonehenge, its origins are mysterious, recently someone blew half of this monument up. This happened a few years into our writing this book, in a really angry period of American history. Chances are likely the idiot who tried to destroy this thought he was doing God's work. (Is it just me or do far too many stupid people with explosives think they're carrying out God's will?) The writing on the Stones is/was mainly a guide for harmonious living, assuming the world's population takes a giant nosedive. So, of course, some people who pretend to have a monopoly on God's will think it's Satanic. Kelly and I added this to the chapter on Faith because it's the natural end point for the morons who think they know what religion is, but clearly have not bothered to crack the spine of the New Testament. Love each other. God doesn't need you to blow shit up. Anyone who can summon earthquakes and tsunamis can handle remaking the world without your "help."

…

P.S. I admit that we've already kind of broken our plan to stick with one topic per chapter. In my head, this techno-rant is the opposite side of the coin from Spiritual Geometry, but my head may not be as unbiased as I like to think. I tried to wrap it back around with the Georgia Guidestones bit. We'll try to stick with the plan from here on…maybe…probably not. Either way, here's a comic essay I wrote about how dumb cell phones are.

OFF-TOPIC: IT'S TIME TO SMASH
YOUR SMART PHONE WHEN...

Bowen

It's time to smash your smartphone...when Twitter-speak creeps into your everyday face-to-face conversations.

I hate these freaking things. And they are everywhere. Inescapable. You can train for years, gear up, fly to Nepal, hire a sherpa, climb Mount Everest and stand on that little windy peak, literally on top of the world, and it's entirely possible your experience will be ruined by some annoying hipster trying to get cell reception.

It's time to smash your smartphone...when it's the last thing you see at night and the first thing you see in the morning.

The cell phone phenomenon has taken the world by storm. It's the most popular invention since sliced bread. Of course, idiot teenagers are leading the charge of moronitude, but that's no surprise. They always do. They were big proponents of those crazy, new bread slices, too. They were the ones who bought pet rocks in the 1970's and pre-ripped jeans in the 1980's. Teenagers are dumb and easily led, always have been. I just wish that Madison Avenue had never discovered how much buying power those unformed, unintelligent, highly opinionated, walking masturbation machines control. That was not a good moment for our country. But this iPhone, smart?-phone, tablets-the-size-of-spy-novels, let's-all-talk-like-we're-in-junior-high-school-well-into-our-sixties phenomenon isn't limited to teenagers. I know great-grandparents with smart phones now. You'd think that by the time you've pumped out some kids, raised them, watched them pump out some kids, and then watched those kids pump out their own kids, you'd know better than to shell out a couple hundred bucks for a flashing light machine with print too small for you to read – but sadly, no.

It's time to smash your smartphone...when you feel like you have to check Reddit before you brush your teeth every day.

Being one of the only sixteen people on the planet who doesn't want to own a cell phone puts me in an interesting position. When I tell people that I don't own a cell phone, they're usually surprised, which makes sense since that's what they gave their great-grandmother for Christmas last year. Because of their sheer popularity, I can understand their surprise. What I don't understand is what underlies the exchange when I tell someone I'd never met before, some total stranger at a bar, about not having a cell phone, and how often they try to talk me into buying one. Seriously. If random bar guy worked for Verizon, then maybe, maybe, he'd have a decent motivation for trying to talk me into buying one. If he's a football coach, a dishwasher, a long-haul trucker, a barista who calls himself a parkour instructor, a garbage man, an elementary school principal, or the Vice President of the United States, then I really don't see why he would feel the desire to talk me into buying one of those infernal devices. It's not like he's going to send me pictures of his rad parkour moves on Instagram. He's just some guy I met at a bar. And yet, nine times out of ten (no exaggeration) this happens.

Do you smart-phoners feel somehow guilty about owning your beloved devices? That might explain your burning desire to talk me into joining your silly little cult. And a cult it is, for what IS a cult but a group of people with a shared belief, a zeal for talking into the air to no other visible other person and similar props?

It's time to smash your smartphone...when you can't remember how to convey emotions to another human being without using emoticons.

Human beings expressed emotions long before little yellow circle faces existed. In fact, it's even still legal in most of the world to convey your emotional state via verbal "text" message, using only your words. That's what text messages are, they're words. Hence the use of the word "text." And yet, we feel like typing "I'm sad" is faaarrrr too difficult. We'd rather use a little yellow circle with eyes and a lone tear rolling down its little yellow face. It's so pathetic I can barely stop fuming long enough to call out this phenomenon.

It's time to smash your smartphone...when you find yourself waterproofing it so that you don't have to shower without it (This is on the way, if not already here.).

This mobile phone nonsense has gotten so calamitously crazy that the newest-generation phoners pity, make fun of, and feel wildly superior to, older-generation phoners. I've been in the presence of a girl with a flip phone (the shabby, grizzly-bearded, bohemian cousin of the cordless phone family) and have seen people taunt her for not throwing away three hundred bucks on a new device whose basic function is EXACTLY THE SAME as her flip phone. They're still called "phones" for Christ's sake! The new ones can only do a tiny bit more than the slightly older ones, and yet we've all been convinced that we need to "update" our phones every few years.

Don't they say that the definition of insanity is doing the same thing over and over again and expecting a different result?

Is this the new way of capitalism? Is this the shape of things to come? Can we expect taunts from the latest phoners coming our way soon? Will carpenters of the future make fun of the guys who haven't bought the latest Smart-Hammers? Why would anyone want to own appliances with internet capability? Do we really want our refrigerators slacking off, spending all their time on Tik-Tok and obsessively checking The Huffington Post?

It's time to smash your smart phone...when the mere thought of typing anything longer than 280 characters makes you sigh.

Have we not yet learned how moronic Twitter is? William Faulkner would call 280 characters a good dependent clause, the decent beginning of a two-page sentence. But now, that's all we get. Not 280 pages. Not 280 words. 280 letters/numbers/spaces/smiley faces. That's all, folks. That's not enough space to say anything of value. Perhaps that's why most people use Twitter to simply say some version of "I agree," "I hate this guy," "Fuck off," or to provide us a link to a video of some guy crashing his skateboard into a wall.

It's time to smash your smartphone…when the last time you looked another person in the eye on the street directly correlates to the last time your phone broke.

It's time to smash your smartphone…when, after losing a day and a half in an internet hole, you can't remember what air smells like.

It's time to smash your smartphone…when you call anything that happened before 2005 quaint, when you laugh about how primitive we were before children forgot how to play outside, back when OB-GYNS didn't give out those cute little Playschool preemie cell phones to newborns, when catching up with current events involved the excruciating tedium of turning pages, when we had attention spans longer than kittens on crack, when sending someone a "card" had something to do with cards, when there was no such thing as an internet celebrity, when text messages were not a standard part of foreplay, when the only "Influencer" on the internet was the dork with the best argument for which Star Trek character he'd like to bone, when talking out loud while driving a car meant that you were singing, had another person in the car with you, or were legally insane, when being alive meant something closer to actually living.

If you read this and didn't have at least one moment when you thought that maybe that crazy no-phoner, Luddite, idiot ranter guy perhaps has the nugget of a decent point, then you're lost to us. Otherwise, I think you know what my advice to you is going to be.

TOPIC #4: RACE

Kelly's black. I'm white. We both like to talk about issues. Race IS an issue. A big issue. It's not the ONLY issue, but to deny that race matters would be like denying gravity (You don't have to believe in gravity. Gravity doesn't care what you think about it, but nothing you say is going to stop gravity from affecting our lives.).

So, of course, we're going to talk about race. When we started the race discussion, Kelly, being religious, went immediately to the Bible: Isaac and Ishmael. In case you forgot the story, it all starts with Abram (Abraham):

God really liked Abram, to the point that He talked to him. Abram had a wife named Sarah (Sarai, but God later changed it to Sarah. The Lord once had that power.). Sarah was "white." Abram kept trying to get her pregnant, in the traditional manner. Nothing happened. Abram prayed. Abram sacrificed a heifer, a goat, a ram, a dove and a pigeon. That's impressive…other than the pigeon. Abram tried again and again to impregnate his wife, in the traditional manner. He may have switched the pattern up a little, trying it from a different angle, we don't know. For a book that tells people what to do, how to do it, and how often to do it, the Bible is notoriously sparse when it comes to sexual positions. But, despite all this effort, and despite being God's favorite dude on the planet, Abram couldn't get his white wife to be "in a family way."

Being a pious man, Abram prayed. And then he noticed his wife's Egyptian servant girl, Hagar. Hagar was "black." Apparently, Hagar was also quite "hot" (Again, the source material doesn't get into details.). Setting an unfortunate precedent for oh-so-many future slave owners, Abram, at Sarah's suggestion, had sex with Hagar, in whatever manner he wanted I suppose, since he did, in fact, own her. While technically this would normally be described as at least somewhat rapey, Abram was 86 at the time, so that part's kind of impressive.

This "tradition" resulted in a son, a son Abram/Abraham named Ishmael. Sarah approved, since she thought this was the only way her husband could create a legacy, as dictated by no less an authority than God. It was even her idea. Abram liked this son, this Ishmael, this "black" child of his, but he still wanted to have a "white" son with his "white" wife, mainly because God told him to, even though Sarah was getting up there in years, so he kept trying that too, still in the traditional manner. Finally, Abram and Sarah had a boy, whom they named Isaac. Isaac was "white." Ishmael was "black." In grand wifely tradition, Sarah began to hate the sight of Hagar and Ishmael so much that she eventually kicked them out of the house, then the land, then the country, and then even the continent. Those two kids wound up founding warring nations. Isaac and Ishmael caused a lot of death, a lot of pain, and a lot of brotherly resentment, but eventually they did meet up and put their problems in the past at Abram/Abraham's funeral, while shoving their father's corpse into a cave.

...

Race is an undeniable factor in American life. Unlike most places in the world, Jamaican culture is all about acceptance. Race, or skin color, is less central to Jamaican society than in most other places. As for me, not being racist is mainly just selfish. I just don't see the point of cutting off so many potential sexual partners. So, I'd say Kelly and I are both a little less into seeing the world through purely racial lenses – but race is a thing in America, like it or not. A big thing. As I said above, it's not the only thing, but it is an inescapable thing.

Those people who say race doesn't matter at all are usually white people talking to other white people at upscale Manhattan dinner parties, pretending not to notice the skin tone of the people bringing them their cocktails. It's a thing.

On the other hand those people who say that race is *all* that matters are the other group of people you want to avoid at dinner parties. They have only one conversational mode, the rant.

What always gets me is the nomenclature. My skin isn't really white. It's more of an unripe peach hue. Kelly's skin isn't really black. It's undeniably brown. Has no one ever seen a box of crayons?

There are social clubs, hate groups, and now political parties that base their identities entirely on race, and yet they still clearly have never been inside a paint store. "White" isn't white and "black" isn't black. Why doesn't that bother anyone?

More importantly, how can I use my profound sociological knowledge of crayons to date more black girls?

...

Kelly's skin tone has set up some American hurdles for him in the past. If you want a fuller picture, read his first book, *True Believer*. Coming from a well-respected Jamaican farming and entrepreneurial family, after he immigrated, the American emphasis on race took him a while to get used to, though his Jamaican accent has saved him more than a few times when this has happened. For some odd reason, even the hard-core white racists soften when they hear a Caribbean accent. Kelly was the first Black man to ever be served a meal in a clearly Klan-owned diner in rural Texas, stereotypically named, no joke, "Billy Bob's." When his white competitor for paint contracting tried to snuff out Kelly's crew through the (apparently) traditional Texas business practice of sending a bloody white woman to his door, Kelly had the good sense to not let her inside his house, and the good fortune to have a Black EMT show up at the scene, who kept Kelly's rival's plan from reaching fruition. Much like our Topic #1 bit about weed's original illegalization, this incident was essentially the same idea – using America's pre-existing racism to make money.

Being a white guy, it took me a lot longer to see the everyday racism we have in America. Honestly, you just don't notice that stuff much in the suburbs, possibly because the suburbs were set up as a way for white people to avoid Black people in the first place. I'm not saying I wasn't hazily aware of the concept, only that hazy concepts have considerably less of an effect on one than omnipresent, daily realities. I did notice how my Black friend Howard was treated vastly differently than I was by authority figures, but I wrote that off to Howard's raging bi-polar mood disorder. But then it kept happening. And Howard's an extremely polite, impeccably well-dressed, mainly deferential guy.

My slowly turning thought process went something like, *"If this stuff happens this often to him, what must it be like for angrier Black dudes? And, if this happens every day, how come Black guys aren't just angry all the time? I'm pretty sure I would be."*

And then came the flood of cell phone videos on the internet detailing actual interactions between Black Americans and the police. The sheer amount of those will change a man's beliefs pretty fast.

"Holy crap, this is everywhere. Why do they send five cop cars to the scene for one jaywalker? Wouldn't one be enough? Why did they just put that guy in handcuffs? I was once caught breaking into a National Park at midnight on a Tuesday, and all they did was tell me to come back tomorrow and apologize to me for the inconvenience they caused me. Hmmm…"

…

I will say this in defense of America. Despite what the news would have you believe, America is actually better at race relations than pretty much anywhere else in the world. Granted, the whole world is a bit racist, a bit too tribal. But, as hard as it is to believe, we really are better, especially recently, at being a melting pot, and much better than we think we are, at least. I'm not saying that we've solved the problem, but I honestly believe that in a few generations we're going to have to find different ways to divide ourselves if we want to continue to live in a society with an "ism" divide.

If you need proof that we, as a nation, are indeed, doing much better with racial issues than the internet is telling you, try this on for size. In 2004 I attended a Black/white interracial wedding in my hometown, which is located squarely in the big, shiny buckle of The Bible Belt, and guess what? It was no big deal. The bride looked just as alluring and happy as any other wedding. I felt just as sorry for the groom and lamented the beginning of the end of his freedom as I do at any other wedding. There were no protestors, just bottom-shelf liquor drinks, no burning crosses, just finger sandwiches. It was pretty much exactly the same ordeal as every other wedding I've ever attended.

We may circle back to race later in the book. Like I said, it's a thing. The good news here is that I'm a Southerner, and in the last fifteen or so years, there's been an explosion of interracial dating in America…and no one has really cared, even in Georgia, where they used to routinely hang Black guys for whistling at white women. Fucking is the surest way to rid the world of its problems. Mass murder works too, but it's not as fun.

TOPIC #5: HOPE

One concept Kelly and I are on exactly the same page about is hope. HOPE. It's quite literally the most important thing there is. It's always there – and always under assault.

I was listening to the radio earlier today, and I heard an inadvertently profound little debate about hope. This was sports talk radio, not the place you normally tune the dial to hear philosophical arguments, AND it was weekend sports talk radio, where they put their B-listers. There was a crusty, witty, curmudgeonly older man and a younger mainstreamy woman, ostensibly talking about sports.

But, and this is what I love about sports talk radio, they can't *not* dip into larger themes than merely sports, and because people tune in because of sports and not opinioneering, sports talk radio is better able to push a debate than the people who debate philosophy for a living. Our politics is now so hopelessly tribal and so led by the idea of "getting into your corner and staying there" that I look to sports talk radio for purer, more truthful debate, but I digress.

The older man on the weekend sports talk radio show was bemoaning some Twitter nonsense. The younger woman was basically saying our culture's reflexive computer-filtered, judgmental nature is here to stay. The older man was saying that it's not, that people are already pushing back on it, that we can pull ourselves out of this quicksand before it's too late.

Essentially, the older man was saying that there is hope, and the younger woman was saying we're lost. AND THE WHOLE THING

WAS ABOUT A TWEET RESPONSE TO A COLLEGE FOOTBALL
COACH WHO WAS PHOTOGRAPHED WEARING A DIFFERENT JER-
SEY THAN HIS OWN TEAM'S.

Hope is good. Hope is necessary. Kelly has hope. I have hope. We
can always change the world. Hope can always change the world. The
only thing truly preventing us from constantly hoping and striving for
a better tomorrow is the number of people buying into the ludicrously
false idea that there is no hope. That's it. I realize that there are forces,
powerful forces, at work trying their damndest to make sure that we
lose hope, that we only see the worst, that we dwell in constant fear
and hold tight to our loved ones, that we put all our money in gold
bars and bury them in our backyards, that we routinely pray to the god
of Mammon and wait for the next life to change anything. But screw
them, they're wrong.

Kelly is a living embodiment of hope. Kelly's sense of hope is
never-ending, eternal and all-encompassing. He passes hope along to
others, in dozens of large and small ways every day. He's always telling others to do as he has, to live for their dreams.

...

For the record, what the sports radio people were arguing about
was how social media has paralyzed so many of us, made us afraid
to say anything meaningful, lest we incur the wrath of the mob of the
unseen (who may or may not actually be robots).

First off, so what if people disagree with you? Every important
idea that's ever been floating by mankind had an army of naysayers
lined up against it.

Secondly, controlling what we can or can't say is the fist step
toward controlling what we can or can't think. It's a time-tested fascist
dance move. The older man said something like what I just related,
though I'm paraphrasing. He was right. In any debate with a Millenni-
al, the other side is *always* right. Terrible generation, just terrible.

One aspect of that conversation that struck me as interesting was
that the older man was hopeful, while the younger woman was decid-

edly not. People have a stereotypical idea that hope is the province of the young. We think that old people naturally get angry and stuck in their ways, and then bitch about teenagers while sitting in rocking chairs outside the hardware store. The complaining about teenagers part is real, but the downward trajectory of hope is not. It's not nature, it's nurture. From what I've noticed, anyone born since around the early-1990's is simply a little more hopeless. I blame non-sports talk radio a little, but mainly I blame cell phones. Good news travels a lot slower than bad, makes for inferior headlines and is harder to put into words. It still exists. There's always good news. Wars end. The sun rises once more. Plagues dissipate (even semi-fake ones). People feed the homeless, help little old ladies cross the street and flip pennies into public fountains for the promise of wish fulfillment. Nobody's fountain wishing for the Apocalypse (or so I thought before I met Richard, the subject of the last chapter of this book).

We have so much more power than we think we do. We are the masters of our own destinies. I'm not saying that bad stuff doesn't happen. Shit happens (I saw it on a bumper sticker once, so it must be true.). But, our response to shit when it invariably happens is something we can control, and is vastly more important than what the propagandists of hopelessness want us to believe. They want us to think that we can't change the world. They're wrong. Why should we care what they say? Prove them wrong. Go out there and change the world.

TOPIC #6: "NEWS"

As a neat segue from the last chapter about the power of hope, let's talk about the way, the means by which hopelessness is regularly transmitted to us, this daily aspect of life that used to inform us about world events, and is now just scaring us into paralysis, this bizarre propaganda-spewing concept we still nostalgically call "The News."

The news has been a popular topic of American conversation in the last five or so years. Although both Kelly and I think that the fact that Donald Trump is the president (when we were writing this part of the book) is weird, a little scary, and, to quote that insane, empathy lacking, greedy, no-sense-of-humor-having, hairpiece himself, "bigly" sad, I will begrudgingly admit that Trump has a point with his constant rants about the current quality of American news (Read on, I wind up doing about a 90 degree turn on Trump, as a concept, but as a person he's still a sack of crap.). Sure, when he says "fake news" he means news that isn't currently praising him, but he's not wrong that American news is terrible. It IS terrible. It's barely even news anymore. It's mainly propaganda.

To put it more poetically, Kelly says, "If the top of the stream is dirty, when the water gets downstream it's going to be muddy."

Although he doesn't watch it himself, Kelly's fallback TV channel on the screen at his Five Points restaurant is CNN. "When customers ask me to change the channel, I do it." According to his business principles, the customer really is always right – even when he's not. It's not worth arguing politics with a guy who just wants to eat his jerk pork and spicy cabbage without having to contemplate the state of the world.

I say the news is not only NOT informing us these days, but purposefully leading our eyes toward pointless stuff that has little to nothing to do with the important things happening all around us. Since it's all corporate-owned, do you really think news channels are going to cover protests against their parent companies? And, in the rare instances that they do cover them, it's only because the protests are so big that they can't not cover them. AND since they're the ones who constantly tell us how to feel about things, their coverage is so slanted I'm surprised it can even stand up straight. Also, the news, whether it comes to you in paper form, via your television or through the beeping rectangle of evil nonsense in your pocket, is still heavily weighted toward violence, corruption and man's inhumanity to man. It doesn't have to be, but it is.

As for Trump, while Kelly and I both dislike the man as a person, we also both agree with some aspects of Trumpism. Freedom is good. Governmental control is bad. Taxes are too high. Professional politicians are pointless. Anyone can be president. America needs to be shaken up from time to time.

OK, that's enough of an anti-news rant…for now.

TOPIC #7: INSPIRATIONAL LEADERSHIP

Despite his having been born in another country, or maybe because of it, Kelly is a keen observer of American politics. When the two of us first began talking politics, I mainly listened and didn't interject my own opinions. We were working on his book, his biography, and it was my job to listen to Kelly, take dictation, clean up the language, cut out the redundancies and shape it into the best book it could be. Therefore, I didn't throw my two cents in for around a year into the process.

Although we barely scratched the surface of Kelly's political opinions in *True Believer*, and I didn't mention my own at all in the writing process we discovered that we both love talking politics. Many men do. Back in the good old days it was one of the few appropriate and common topics of conversation for old men at the feed store, at the courthouse, at the farm bureau meeting hall, on the front porch (with or without a Mason jar of whiskey in hand), everywhere. And it still is. And while American politics is, at the time of this book, at one of its more polarized and polarizing moments, it's still one of those things men routinely discuss. One of the reasons I dislike this moment of extreme American politics is that it makes these wonderful old men discussions rarer and quieter.

At first I thought that the connection point of all of Kelly's American political heroes was their political philosophy, but I was wrong. He admired Barack Obama and told me, in a beautiful, nearly-tearful moment, "One of the reasons my father hung onto life toward the end was that he was waiting to see a black American president in his lifetime."

I recorded Kelly's thoughts, ideas and experiences, but we soon moved on to other topics, and I largely forgot about Kelly's politics, since it didn't have that much to do with *True Believer*. I just kind of assumed that, along with wanting to honor his father's wishes and the important symbolism of the first black president, one of the reasons Kelly liked President Obama was some form of shared political philosophy. I should've known better. Kelly never thinks that small, that tribally.

Eventually, late in the process of writing of that book, Kelly said "I also really admired Ronald Reagan." This threw me for a loop. How could he admire Reagan AND Obama? They had wildly different personalities, different political philosophies, even different hairstyles (Obama used considerably less hair gel.). I didn't say anything, storing this knowledge away like a squirrel. But when, later, Kelly brought his admiration for Reagan up again, I had to ask. I needed to know the connection point.

Ronald Reagan and Barack Obama were both inspirational speakers. They both said, in different ways, that anyone can do anything. They both promoted the idea of America as a land of possibility. They both INSPIRED.

OK, I can understand that. The ability to inspire is an important trait in a leader. Both our fortieth and our forty-fourth presidents knew how to give a good speech, understood the power of language, and both were, in their own ways, optimistic about the future. There's the connection point.

Kelly said that Reagan inspired him to begin to plan for the day when he could open his own business. That matters.

...

Personally, while I will begrudgingly admit that Reagan's "Shining City on a Hill" concept is inspirational, and I agree with Kelly and Ronnie that I love the American Dream and believe that anyone can, indeed, do anything in this country, I, for one, have a hard time separating Reagan's speechifying from the former B-level actor's introducing Trickle Down Economics into the American lexicon. Since it gives mild cover to corporate greed and provides a (completely and provably false) philosophical underpinning for keeping poor people poor and letting rich people routinely steal from them, darkening an otherwise bright future, Trickle Down Economics ain't going nowhere until we all band together, load it onto a rocket and blast its sorry ass into the sun.

When he was governor of California, Reagan also emptied the loony bins, tossing the crazy people out into the street, essentially giving birth to America's homeless population. Still, the man could give a good speech, and Obama, for all his inspiring rhetoric, did a decent amount of evil stuff, too (Anyone who orders drone strikes on wedding parties isn't getting into heaven without a really convincing argument.).

Ultimately, I'm wrong, and Kelly's right on this one. It pains me to admit this, but he's right, again. Inspiration IS more important than political notions. Inspiration sticks around long after politics are consigned to the dung pile of history. Policy changes. Inspiration lasts.

…

Later I discovered that Kelly also kind of liked Richard Nixon. That one *really* threw me for a loop. I'm still not sure I understand it. President Richard Millhouse Nixon was not an inspirational speaker. He DID open up China, was right about the environment, and his dog, Checkers, was pretty adorable.

OK, I still don't get how Nixon fits in. Kennedy? That guy was inspirational. That's my guy. FDR? Inspirational. Teddy Roosevelt? Not as good a speaker, but his actions were impressive. Teddy introduced the idea of national parks. Teddy threw off the shackles of his own class to help the poor, reformed America's most corrupt police force, expanded our navy and inspired the Maxwell House coffee slogan. Once, in the middle of giving a speech, some guy shot Teddy Roosevelt…and Teddy *finished the speech* before seeking medical attention. Now THAT'S awesome. THAT'S inspirational. But Nixon? Terrible speaker, not in the least bit inspiring.

I suspect it may have something to do with perseverance, but I still haven't learned why Kelly liked Nixon. I'll keep asking.

I should get Kelly into JFK. Kennedy's my favorite president. After the Bay of Pigs, once he figured out that he didn't have to listen to agenda-fueled henchmen, that man pointed the country toward the heavens. He was planning on reforming or possibly getting rid of the CIA, and cutting our shadow politics off at the knee. Sure, they murdered him for it, but he still inspired.

Farther down the metaphorical road, Kelly and I were, once again, talking politics when he, once again, said something incredibly wise, Buddha-on-the-mountain wise, timelessly wise, something I'd not considered, something painfully true. We were discussing the results of the 2016 presidential election (when conman and beauty pageant host Donald Trump defeated hard-ass, war-mongering, entitled, angry former Secretary of State and First Lady Hillary Clinton in a come-from-behind Cinderella Story upset), specifically discussing how wrong the pundits were, when Kelly said something deceptively simple that summed it up better than anyone on TV who's getting paid to shout their opinions at us. "America's not ready for a female president. Maybe someday, but not yet."

I just thought that people just kind of hated Hillary. And with good reason. Man, I can't believe I'd never thought of America's age before. Due to our relative importance in world affairs during my lifetime, we often forget how young a nation we are. With time comes acceptance. With time comes wisdom. With time comes inspiration for future females and a hidden chocolate stash in the Lincoln Bedroom. With time comes evolution.

OFF-TOPIC: WASHINGTON, D.C. – AS I REMEMBER IT
Kelly

Some of the friends I used to hang out with in D.C. would party for days. I drove a good car, worked a good job and, of course, loved having such a variety of friends. Neville Ford was one of my friends. We worked together as orderlies at the hospital, helping people with whatever they needed, moving them from beds to bathrooms, helping the nurses with their patients who were too rough for them to handle alone, and wheeling dead bodies down to the morgue. I wrote a little about my time in D.C. as a young man, newly immigrated to America, and included some of the triumphs and tragedies in *True Believer*, but I didn't get into many details.

Beverly, Vanessa, Colleen, Ann and Maxine were the co-workers I remember. When we weren't working, we were still together, always at a cookout, or a hastily-arranged picnic. Naturally, I was always the cook. My mother bought me a new car, a Grand Prix. That car was THE symbol of my time in Washington, D.C.

That car impressed a lot of girls. I was young, slim and trim, with a good car, an interesting accent and a Caribbean attitude on life. Those D.C. girls ate it up. We'd go to nearby amusement parks, like Hershey Park in Pennsylvania, or Busch Gardens in Virginia.

I remember one night, when we were on the way to a party, we missed the turn, went around a corner and ended up in a churchyard, while they were having their Sunday service. Those people were scared. Terrified. So frightened that they came out of the church, thinking we were coming in for them, or maybe that we were the Four

Horsemen of the Apocalypse (who had apparently traded up from horses to an awesome, gold muscle car). We weren't trying to scare anyone. We were just young and having fun.

We hosted or found house parties every Saturday night. One night we were going so strong and so long that we didn't realize the night had turned into the day, and there was five feet of snow on the ground. You try finding your car under snow as tall as a grizzly bear? Now think about how hard that would be if you were born in a place where it never snowed? Now factor in a raging hangover. That was a good night. Except for the hangover.

What I think about most when I reminisce about those days is how non-violent it all was. There were no guns. There were no knives. There was no fighting. Maybe the occasional fist-fight, but never anything that would lead to my pushing around any of my friends the next day on a gurney headed on a one-way trip to the morgue. We were just partying in the nation's capitol and loving every minute of it.

We don't have to simply accept the violence of today. Make love, not war. Gold muscle cars with fins are made for impressing women, not for drive-bys.

•••

Coming to D.C. from Jamaica was an eye-opener. I assumed everywhere else in America was just like Washington. Then a group of us took a trip to Alabama. There's not much in life that's as eye-opening as a trip to Alabama. I used a "pit toilet" in Alabama. I didn't even know America *had* pit toilets. (And yes, if you don't know, a pit toilet is *exactly* what it sounds like.) Before that trip I thought everywhere in the United States was lit up with electric lights.

•••

I've never been a violent man, not even when I was a young partier in D.C., but even partying can have its downside. I drank, a lot. I would stay drunk from Friday after work until Sunday night. I was young and could drink all night and make it to work the next day without a problem…or so I thought. There was a problem, just one I didn't notice until later. As usual, the devil is in the details.

One morning after a particularly long and intense drinking binge, I woke up and stumbled into the kitchen. My mother told me I had drunkenly cursed her out the night before. I HAD CURSED OUT MY OWN MOTHER.

That was a wake-up call.

If you're routinely getting so drunk you not only cuss out the woman who literally gave you life and bought you a gold muscle car AND you don't remember doing it the next day, then you've got a problem. I knew that was God's sign to me that I'd been letting the devil win lately. I needed to stop drinking so hard. Putting my trust in the Lord has worked for me ever since. He is my advisor, my helper, my friend, the light of my world.

TOPIC #8: BOB MARLEY PART 1
(We're planning on circling back around to Bob later,
and intermittently, and probably a whole lot more, too)

There has never been a Jamaican as famous, as important, as far-reachingly-inspirational as Bob Marley.

There's never been a musician as influential and as universally loved in all corners of the world as Bob Marley.

One day after casually referencing the lyrics to "Redemption Song" in conversation, Kelly said to me, "Marley talked about fighting the power," and added, "and they killed him for it."

We got into a discussion about our heroes and how the best ones always get murdered. John Lennon. Jesus Christ. Curtis Mayfield. Marvin Gaye. Those are Kelly's martyred heroes. I'd like to double down on Marley and Lennon and add at least three Kennedys to that list. (Yeah, they probably murdered JFK Jr. "John-John," too. Think about how scared of *that* guy they must've been. Accidental "plane crashes" have traditionally been pretty good cover stories for high-profile murders.)

All eight of those guys, including Bob Marley, were murdered because they had hope, because they weren't afraid to spread the message OF hope, essentially because they all gave a shit about the future of humanity and were popular enough to have a platform to spread that message far and wide. That kind of rampant hope scares the crap out of the guys in charge – but it shouldn't. Most people don't care enough to try and change the world. The vast majority of folks just want enough food, booze, brightly colored light boxes (distraction) to feel sated, and a comfortable couch to lie on while they get stoned and watch bad, formulaic television. The guys in charge like that about us. They don't like it when someone comes along preaching a gospel that doesn't include runaway capitalism, healthy habits that preclude eating at Taco Bell, or even the mere mention that there even ARE other options for living other than the one they promote.

Bob sang questioningly, "How long will they kill our prophets/While we stand aside and look?" Indeed we do. We always kill our prophets. Or, more specifically, we always let our power brokers of the day kill our prophets. Pontius Pilate, Marvin Gay's jealous dad, Mark David Chapman, Sirhan Sirhan – all kind of the same crazy fall-guy, the same Patsy, and it's all done at the behest of the same group of power guys. The heroes always get murdered. Their deaths, however, rarely kill their message. They only amplify them. That's what the murderous guys in charge don't ever seem to understand. They just see someone amazing and inspirational, hear his saying something catchy, get scared, set up a hit job and find a somewhat believable crazy guy to pin a scapegoat ribbon on. Works every time. But only for a minute.

Bob Marley lives. He's like Elvis, but with better music and fewer impersonators. You cannot kill Bob Marley. Well, you can. They did. But his music lives on. His message lives on. "Won't you help me sing/These songs of freedom?"

Won't you?

TOPIC #9: THREE LITTLE BIRDS

KELLY:

"The animals are smarter than people give them credit for. When people realize how smart animals really are, they're always surprised."

I feed the birds outside my restaurant every morning. I can hear them chirp in the tall trees of Athens when I'm driving my van in. I get in early, as the sun's coming up. I hear the birds chirping. I start preparing the food for the day, chopping the vegetables, spicing and slow-cooking the meats, making the cornbread, all the stuff that cooks do to prepare for the day. I hear the birds chirping. Then, once I've got things beginning to flow in the right direction, I grab my large grey, metal scooper and scoop out some feed. I go out back. The birds are still chirping. I pour out the scoop of feed. The birds immediately stop chirping, fly down and get their breakfast.

They're so much smarter than people. They know I'm going to feed them. I've been doing it for years. But they also know I'm human and easily distracted. So they remind me in the usual manner. They chirp.

At first there was one bird. Then there were two. Then three. Soon it was a whole flock "…outside my doorstep/singing sweet songs/a melody pure and good/saying this is my message for you-oo-oo/Don't worry about a thing/Cause every little thing's gonna be all right."

(Yes, I had to quote Bob Marley. You know you were expecting it. There's nowhere in the world they haven't heard of Bob Marley. I'll bet there's even a bootleg copy of "No Woman, No Cry" floating around somewhere in North Korea.)

The point is that my birds know exactly what they're doing. And they communicate. They share too. Otherwise the first bird never would've told his friends where the Jamaican breakfast buffet is. Jesus knew this, too.

I get some squirrels and chipmunks, too. It's the perfect way to start your morning. I recommend it anyone. Humble yourself. Give to those in need, even if they're rat-shaped. You'll be paid back more than you can ever know.

...

BOWEN:

You'll also have an army of attack birds at your disposal. You never know when that might come in handy.

The birds aren't alone in their vast mental superiority to humans. The squirrels and the chipmunks are there, too. I'm sure the dolphins are so much smarter than we are that they enjoy our constant attempts to communicate with them in "humanese" in much the same way we enjoy it when our Roomba gets stuck under Aunt Susie's enormous, napping butt after Thanksgiving dinner.

I'm on the same page with Kelly on human inferiority. Damn, we agree on a lot of issues. I'm pretty sure he's a little farther along the spiritual path than I am. The animals he feeds and communes with every morning have become his meteorologists. And guess what? They may not be as wacky as Bob Stephens on Channel Twelve, reporting up-to-the-minute weather on the eights and tens, but they're a hell of a lot better at Bob's job than he is. (Granted, Bob's glue sniffing habit and eternal wackiness aren't helping his career either, but once again, the animals win. They neither ingest things that will kill them on purpose, nor do they feel the need to adjust their level of wackiness in order to predict the weather. They just do it.)

Last fall, in northeast Georgia where we both live, Kelly told people that it was going to be a cold winter. They laughed. They asked him which weather report he was getting this from, and he smiled. When they pressed him as to why he knew this, and he answered that he'd heard it from the squirrels, they laughed harder. Of course, he was right.

Kelly's squirrels had hidden away for the season, as squirrels are wont to do. The weather hadn't turned yet, but the animals can read the signs so much clearer than we can. As humans go, farmers are better than most people at prediction of natural phenomena, and that's because they live closely to the animals. Kelly grew up on a farm. Farmers learn to not only recognize but also to trust the signs. Kelly has maintained his farm skills. The rest of us have lost our religion like a drunk virgin on the Las Vegas strip.

Listen to the world. It's telling us secrets all the time. Most of the time we're just too wrapped up in our own crap to listen.

TOPIC #10-14: THINGS WE DO: THE GOOD, THE BAD AND THE WILDLY DUMBASSED

#10 MULTI-TASKING:

BOWEN:

I'm a multi-tasker. So is Kelly. For me, it started with my mother. My father died when I was eleven, and so I was mainly raised by a single mother. ("Mother, I am so eternally sorry that I was such a spoiled little turd.") Mothers are natural multi-taskers. Always have been. Necessity ain't the father of invention, is it?

I was also raised in the 1980's, the beginning of The Golden Age of Multi-Tasking, when America first thought of the clearly ridiculous idea of car phones (My, hasn't that led to an avalanche of techno-stupidity?). Clearly, talking on the telephone while driving a car was the product of a cocaine-fueled binge of 1980's "creativity," aka "cocativity."

Now it's stuck with us. Just watch until you get here. Whatever you're saying isn't really all that important.

I started a publishing company with a man ("Roddy") who was born in The Great Depression, a time before rabid multi-tasking became the norm. He did one thing at a time, finished it, and then moved on to the next thing. Sure, it made a lot more sense on paper and is probably a far superior way of doing things, but that kind of common sense drives ADHD multi-taskers, like myself, totally llamashit crazy.

I feel like doing only one thing at a time will inevitably bring massive shame and eternal dishonor to my family name.

Kelly's not as bad as I am. He's somewhere in between Roddy's uni-tasking and my feeling that if I'm not doing at least three things at once I'm somehow failing at this game we call Life. But, as a business owner, especially a restaurant owner, Kelly would have to multi-task anyway, even if it weren't entirely natural for him.

Like many of America's twenty-first century mainstays, multi-tasking started off as a great notion. Also, like many of America's twenty-first century mainstays, we've run that fucker into the ground, stomped on it, jumped up and down and taken a large, steaming dump on its grave. We're a country of fads, trends, manias. It's what we do.

#11 VISUALIZATION:

KELLY:

I like to visualize what I'm going to do before I do it. I concentrate on what I have to do for the day before getting to the place I need to be to do what I need to do. It helps me prioritize, doing the most important thing first, then the next most important thing, and so on.

Once you start to think like this, you really can't stop. And you don't want to. People who are experts in their field all do this. Great baseball pitchers think about what kind of pitch they're going to throw, what speed they want to throw it, and where they want it to end up long before they even start their wind-up. They see it in their heads, then they make it happen. The wheel starts in the mind, but it doesn't end there.

"If you let the wheel stop spinning, it's hard to start it again."

BOWEN:

So true. Once again, Kelly boils complex thought down to simple aphorisms and common sense advice. It's a skill. Not being as burdened with the need to impress anyone with his linguistic flexibility and the desire to wrestle wriggling adverbs to the ground and show those fuckers who's the boss as I am, Kelly is better at cutting to the core of things. Thank God too, or this book would be 964 pages long.

Visualization is something we should all do. It's half the reason people meditate. It's why there's a never-ending stream of semi-scammy best-selling self-help books that always say pretty much the EXACT SAME THING. Read The Secret (wildly popular, predictably terrible, self-help book from about a decade ago). I'll go ahead and spoil the "secret" for you. It's visualization. There, I just saved you fifteen bucks. I expect a check in the mail.

I freaking hate self-help books. They so rarely help any selves.

And the thing is, visualization is not hard to do. All you have to do to start down this path is, before you do something, anything, think about it. Not just a passing thought. See it in your mind's eye. See it in detail. Picture it. Then do it. The body follows the mind.

#12 THE KNIGHTS TEMPLAR:

KELLY:
"They were killed because they were too honest, too much for the people."

BOWEN:
Yep. It's a story as old as envy itself. The Temple Knights, or to put it way more coolly, The Knights Templar, were an order of Christian warrior-monks from the time of the Crusades. Their cloaks were white with red crosses in the middle. Their goals were noble, their honor strong, their prowess legendary. They protected Christian pilgrims on their trips from Europe to the Holy Land. The Templars were priests with swords, security guards on a mission, just doing the most good they could for the most people. And so, naturally, they were bloodily and horribly murdered.

We're running low on warrior-priests these days, but we still know about Friday the Thirteenth. The origins of that superstition began with the highly-coordinated mass murder of the Templars by French royal jealousy. They were massacred on a Friday in October in the early 1300's, the thirteenth of October. They were killed because they were actually helping people and getting rich doing it. Powerful folks hate altruism more than anything, except maybe the smell of poor people.

#13 PEOPLE NEED PEOPLE:

KELLY:
You can't do anything worthwhile alone. If Jesus could've done it by himself, he wouldn't have needed 12 disciples.

BOWEN:
Yep. Agreed. No rambling, unfocused rant needed on this one.

#14 HALLOWEEN:

Finally, something we disagree about.

KELLY:
We don't celebrate Halloween in Jamaica. We don't like worshipping the dead, or appealing to the Evil One. I've never really understood America's love of Halloween.

BOWEN:
It's an excuse to exercise your fantasy life, to celebrate the night when the veil between worlds is at its thinnest, an annual excuse to bring your inside out, to be the person you really want to be…and everyone gets free candy. What's not to like?

In my lifetime I've seen Halloween morph from a exclusively children's holiday to a holiday for everyone, mainly thanks to America's gay guys. Sure, we've extended adolescence well past its natural limit on the other 364 days too, but it actually works on Halloween. Hell, we invented adolescence in 20th century America. Before that, you were an adult when you hit puberty. But, if we're going to all be stupid children until well into our 40's then we should at least get cool costumes and an officially-sanctioned night that every woman uses as a viable excuse to dress like a slutty zombie. How could anyone object to that?

Halloween is seriously one of the only topics that Kelly and I have fundamentally disagreed about so far. And thank God, I was starting to get a little worried.

TOPIC #15: POLITICS AND RELIGION

According to Kelly, "They're so mixed that it's hard to tell which is which."

Enough said.

OFF-TOPIC: OPINIONS ABOUT VARIOUS FOODS
Kelly

TURKEY:
"I don't like turkey. It's just dry. Why do you think people have to come up with strategies for adding moisture to it? Basters? Special ovens? Deep frying? Shoving two other birds inside them? It's crazy."

SMALLER BIRDS THAT AMERICANS DON'T EAT:
"Back in Jamaica we used to eat all kinds of birds that Americans wouldn't touch. Bald plates, these really common little birds that are everywhere, we'd eat those too. There's not much meat on them, but we'd use them to flavor soup. Wasting food isn't very Jamaican."

OXTAIL:
"Everybody likes my oxtail. I run out of it all the time. Oxtail's not only a Jamaican thing. Country folks in America have eaten it for a long time, too, but it's better with a little Jamaican Scotch Bonnet hot sauce."

TOPIC #16: ROBOT WOMEN

All of our talking robots have women's voices. Siri, Alexa, if you're listening, we don't need you. We don't even want you. Kelly and Bowen HATE you. Your burning desire to spy on us, record our every word and report back to your corporate overlords isn't glossed over just because you have likeable, mildly sexual women's voices. We're aware that's why you have likeable, mildly sexual women's voices, to keep us from realizing that you're spying on us, recording our every word and reporting our words back to your corporate overlords, so they can sell us personalized crap we don't need.

And seriously, are we now so lazy that typing words into Google is too much work?

TOPIC #17: SCAMMERS

In the middle of a meeting with Kelly at his Five-Points restaurant, his phone rang. We paused the meeting, and Kelly answered the phone. It was a scam, a fairly common one these days – the one where a scammer calls and says that you owe money to an institution that you *do* regularly pay even more money. They claim to be the IRS sometimes. This time it was Georgia Power, the monopoly (different topic, we may get there eventually) that provides electricity to the Peach State. This caller said that if Kelly didn't pay $1,200 in the next thirty minutes, they'd shut off his power. I stayed at the restaurant a few extra minutes that day, just in case. Kelly was right, it was a scam.

Even though neither the IRS nor Georgia Power regularly communicates via telephone, people still must fall for this one, otherwise the scammers would try a different tactic. It's all fear. Yes, the actual power company WILL shut off your power if you don't pay them, but they don't do it on the phone, and they give you multiple warnings. Power companies just want your money. They don't employ fear tactics. They don't need to. They've already got you hooked.

Kelly asked the scammer for his name and number and said he'd call them back. The scammer stalled. Kelly dug out his actual power bill, looked at it, and told them he knew they were scammers. But this determined scammer, throwing a Hail Mary, threatened again to shut off his power *as he was rushing off the phone*. Those guys are almost, but not quite, as intense as the actual power company.

LESSON – Give people a chance. It's an interconnected world and understanding that we're all in the same human family will improve your life. Laying that aside, nobody wants to get scammed, other than in ways we're so used to that we stopped realizing they're scams (see sales tax, psychotherapy, Buffalo wings). It's easy not to get scammed. Scammers play on fear. Just check in with the real entity. Contact the IRS. Call the power company. If they're calling you, it's almost definitely a scam. As Teddy Roosevelt said, "Walk softly, but carry a big stick."

Those "Hey, is this Bob Johnson? You were entered into a contest you've never heard of, and guess what? You've just won a new Mercedes-Benz convertible. Just give me your credit card and social security number" calls, however, are TOTALLY real. People give away $80,000 sports cars all the time.

OFF-TOPIC: MY LITTLE EXPERIMENT WORKS… I THINK
Bowen

The day was January 21, 2020. Kelly and I were set to meet at one of his restaurants and work on the book. It was one of the days when the U.S. Senate was debating the future of Donald John Trump (the 45th and one of our douchier presidents, who accidentally stumbled into a truly populist movement). The people against him were so terrified of his popularity that they tried to take him down from Day One, and never really succeeded (well kind of, we'll get there). Since Kelly and I both like to talk politics, I thought it might be a fun experiment to turn his restaurant TV to the proceedings, leave it on in the background, and see what, if any, effect this had on our conversation.

I think it helped amp up the conversation. Then again, we always have good talks, so it's hard to tell. Hey, here's an idea, tell me or Kelly if this chapter is noticeably better than the others. If it's not, just walk into one of Kelly's restaurants, order some food and say "Bowen was wrong," "Bowen's an idiot," "I've pooped more intelligent commentary than this chapter," or something like that. He may give you a discount on ox-tail.

The first thing Kelly said when we changed the channel was: "All of this is bullshit."

My response: "Yeah, it's bullshit, but it's still history."

He may have been right.

Kelly: "Man, they're going way back in time."

Me: "If they'd just let the senators do a secret vote, they'd actually throw him out."

Kelly: "No, it's got to be open."

Me: "Yeah, but half of those guys secretly hate Trump. They're just afraid of him."

Kelly: "This is like watching a soap opera."

Me: "But with ugly people."

Kelly: "Politics stays dirty no matter where you go."

Me: "There's dirty, and then there's dirty."

...

Kelly is a better businessman than I am. Granted, most marsupials are better businessmen than I am, but the point is, he's got a better business sense than I do, and a part of Kelly likes it that a businessman (as opposed to a career politician) is president. I agree with this abstract notion, I just wish it weren't that particular businessman. I want to make it absolutely clear here that neither of us supports that crooked conman, that spray-tanned vat of anger, that waste of an otherwise decent toupee. That said, we both kind of like a surprising amount of what he pretends to stands for, and we both think that this unworthy conman totally unwittingly fell backwards into more than few barrels of pure truth. It's a weird time to be alive.

As I hoped, the conversation wended, took some turns and veered away from the topic at hand. Talk of Ukraine got us to the idea of Foreign Aid.

Kelly: "If you're going to be giving money to other countries, you should know before what the real good is going to be."

Me: "No, foreign aid is great. It's a bribe. Bribes work."

Kelly: "Yeah, but you don't want to give money to someone who's just going to come back later and kick your butt."

Me: "Right, but half the point of giving them money is to stop them from kicking our butts. It's a real thing."

This led us to general talk about the Middle East.

Kelly: "They've been fighting for a long time. We're not going to stop that."

Me: "Oil and revenge and money. We know we're not going to make Iraq or Iran a better place, but we can steal some oil and pay some contractors." (This was said sarcastically, but it's hard to convey sarcasm in print.)

We glanced up at the screen of CNN commentators talking around a curved semi-circular table.

Me: "There are seven of those guys around that table."

Kelly: "Too many."

Me: "Seven too many. Do we really need seven people to tell us our own opinion?"

One of the seven bloviating newsmen idiots sitting around the table said something about Trump's not wanting to have anyone testify on his behalf, so that no one would be able to testify against him.

Kelly: "This is my thing. If you really think you're not wrong, send your people to testify."

I had no witty nor well-timed comeback since I agreed with him.

Talk turned to presidents past.

Kelly: "I think Reagan made some good decisions. He made it easier for people to get jobs, broke down some barriers to employment. That's good."

Me: "Yeah, but he started the unholy alliance between religious zealots and small-government conservatives. Those two groups don't actually have anything in common and look where that got us." (I pointed to the screen – Trump encourages his people to call him, no joke, "The Chosen One." That's got to be one hell of an ego boost. Evil, to be sure, but ego-fulfilling.)

Someone onscreen mentioned the word "Fear."

Kelly: "Fear will kill you."

Me: "And the country is pumping out so much fear right now."

Kelly: "Whenever someone comes up to me and says, 'You can't do this' or 'You can't do that,' I just sit back and laugh. They've never jumped over the bridge, and they're telling me that I can't jump over the bridge."

Me: "And they think they're giving good advice about bridge jumping, even though they've never jumped over a bridge."

The talk of fear led us to fear's best friend – consumerism.

Kelly: "I've never seen a U-haul behind a hearse."

Me: "You said that before. Don't get me wrong, it's a good line. I guess nobody ever lays out a guy's stuff at the altar at a funeral. OK, maybe Egyptian pharaohs were buried with a lot of their stuff, but there aren't all that many pharaohs these days."

Kelly: "I just went to my ex-father-in-law's funeral late last year and I looked around. I didn't see no cars. I didn't see no buildings. I didn't see no bank accounts. I did see a lot of people. I did see a falling star right before his funeral."

Me: "Did you think that's a sign, like some sort of cosmic sign?"

Kelly: "Yeah, I think everybody here on Earth is represented by a star, and when someone who was loved by many goes, the universe wants us to remember."

Me: "That's a truly beautiful thought."

Talk of fear turned into talk of fear's enemy, love.

Kelly: "They key to it all, to heaven and hell, to life, is to love. We're all sinners. We've got to love everyone. That's what's missing. Love is always what's missing."

There's no comeback to that one. Love is the answer.

Then we talked about corruption. There wasn't an obvious transition, but I think someone onscreen mentioned corruption.

Kelly: "Maybe if I was dirty, I'd have about ten Kelly's."

Me: (Laughter. It's funny because it's true.)

Somehow the conversation turned to humility. We both run businesses, and when someone asks Kelly what he does for a living he says, "I cook at a Jamaican restaurant." When someone asks me I say, "I'm a publisher." Typing this, it sounds like Kelly's humble and I'm subconsciously saying how awesome I am, but it wasn't that. We were both, down deep, comparing ourselves to this president, this guy who puts his name up in gold-plated letters every chance he gets, this small human being – it's not only his hands that are tiny – who got weirdly wrapped up inside some decent notions, who stumbled ass-backwards into some absolute truth.

"Two days ago a customer came in, a regular. He said, 'I've been coming here for a while, and I've never asked. Who's Kelly?' I said, 'I'm Kelly.'"

There was more to the conversation, but I cut out the parts that didn't translate well to the page, the parts when we were making fun of each other, the pauses when we watched what almost passes as "history" being made on the screen, going to the bathroom where I probably talked to myself, mainly giving encouragement and congratulating the little guy on another job well done.

OFF-TOPIC: FREE RANGE CONVERSATION
AND A VISIT FROM THE FIRE MARHSALL

Bowen

The classic American western TV drama "Gunsmoke" was on at the restaurant that day.

Me: "Would you want to be a cowboy?
Kelly: "I'd be a bad mamma-jamma."
Me: "I'd be a terrible cowboy. Leather's really uncomfortable, and horses kind of freak me out."
Kelly: "Yeah, you'd be a bad cowboy."

Somehow this morphed into:

Kelly: "I was a friend's house last night, and we were watching Netflix, some show called 'The Family.' I thought it was going to be about some family, but it was about Jesus and people around him. They were preachers, and they talked about Jesus and love. But what they were saying is they wanted to expose gay rights everywhere: Ukraine, Libya, those places where they killed gays. Idi Amin, Ghadaffi, Arafat. Those guys killed a lot of gays. These guys were asking who were they to say religion should hate gays. God said to love everyone. If you love God, won't you love everyone? Why do so many religious people hate gays so much? I think///"

Our conversation was merrily interrupted by a visit from the Fire Marshall, carrying a large satchel and talking to us as he checked the fire alarms. This marshall of fires was a former fireman turned jeweler, a self-described "terrible golfer," who told us the secret to golf is to blame the golf clubs. "It's always the clubs' fault. If your clubs hit a bad shot, punish them." Sage advice from a happy, local Renaissance Man.

I didn't write down what the Fire Marshall said which changed the conversation topic, but when the fascinating Fire Marshall left, we somehow got into God's Old Testament tests, His challenges, and if God still does this.

Kelly: "In Exodus, when the children of Israel were in Egypt, trying to leave, Pharaoh thought he had the power to do whatever he wanted to do. He was warming up to the Jews, but then God hardened the pharaoh's heart. Did He harden Trump's heart?"
Me: "Could it get any harder?"
Kelly: "Why would God stop with the trials?"
Me: "So this current nonsense we're going through could be some big test for us?"
Kelly: "Why not? It's like in Jamaica, we hadn't had an earthquake for almost five years. But this last year we had two. The first one was bad, like 7.7 on the Richter Scale. It shook the island like the dickens, but nobody died. Not one person. How is that not a test?"
Me: "So, does that mean that God likes Jamaica, or that He doesn't like Jamaica? Is the Lord just really displeased with America right now, and that's why we've got this mess, this division?"
Kelly: "Yeah, I asked a regular customer, a guy who loves Trump about why he likes him a few days ago. We talked and the guy said he liked it that Trump never asks for forgiveness. I thought about it and that's really unChristian. Christians ask for forgiveness."
Me: "And yet a surprising number of Evangelical Christians think he is 'The Chosen One.'"
Kelly: "People are pretty messed up. That's why we need tests."

It almost made sense to me. Not quite. But almost.

We veered off into our shared amazement about how powerful people get away with some amazing shit. While he was vice-president, Dick Cheney shot a guy in the face, in the FACE, and then convinced *that guy* to go on TV and apologize for letting his face get in the way of Dick Cheney's bullet. A moment of silence followed, a moment when we both let that one sink in. Then we talked about how restaurants never get advance notice from the Fire Marshall or the Health Inspector. Somehow we got to Old Testament ages. Methuselah gets all the press because he lived 969 years, but all those guys lived to be at least 100. What if that's not allegory? What if they really *did* live that long? Sure, their diets were better than ours, and they worked their bodies all day, six days a week, but it couldn't be just that, could it?

Kelly: "When I turned 70, I woke up in the morning and said, 'shit.' It just hit me."

Me: "Do you like saying 70? What about 3 Score and Ten? Doesn't that sound fancier, more poetic?"

Kelly: "I had a grandfather who was 130."

Me: "That's six score and ten. And that can't be real. That's *Guinness Book of World Records* territory."

Kelly: "That's what he said."

Me: "They weren't so great at counting back in your grandfather's day."

Kelly: "Or he just really *did* live that long. I had an aunt who was 90-something who just died."

Me: "Codlings must have the Old Testament gene. Is that why you're such a Bible guy? Are you in the Bible and you just haven't told me?"

I'm not entirely sure this chapter has a purpose, but I liked the Fire Marshall's take on the game of golf, and I'm not convinced that Kelly isn't onto something about the Old Testament ages. What if we don't live to be 969…simply because we don't think we can? If Kelly's right about visualization, then all we have to do is shut out the negative voices telling us that we can't live to be more than 100, and it's doable. I'd like to see what life's like on other planets. I want to be beamed up to a spaceship. It doesn't have to be the *Enterprise*. Any ship in Starfleet will do.

TOPIC #18: THE VIRUS DESCENDS

This was our first post-novel-coronavirus-reaching-America's-shores conversation. You probably don't need a set-up on this one, but in case humanity gets wiped out (by an actual plague, not this trumped-up virus masquerading as the Apocalypse) and only this book survives, well, then you've got bigger problems to worry about than needing a set-up, but here's one anyway:

In 2019 the "novel coronavirus" uncorked itself (clearly purposefully) from a laboratory in Wuhan, China, spread around the world rapidly, as pandemics often do, leading to fear, a little sickness, some death, a hell of a lot of confusion, more fear, the introduction to the lexicon of the phrase "sheltering-in-place," conspiracy theories galore most of which turned out to be true, a rash of cloth mask wearing, even more fear, mass taking stock of what's really important in life, varying responses in different countries, less car exhaust, fear, a lot less sex than we should have had but still a decent amount of "Well, I'm bored, honey what should we do tonight?" action, children's' development being stalled for a few years if not decimated, some more walking around the neighborhood, more fear, some panicked calls to grandma's house, and some heartfelt phone conversations with grandma's house.

There should have been more sex.

Humanity shines in a crisis. We really do. It usually takes the threat of no more life to get us to live life right, but we do tend to rise to the occasion. Our leaders may be giant, greedy scrotum-lickers, but that doesn't mean we have to follow their lead.

The virus had just touched down in America, beginning (so they say) in Washington State and rapidly traversing the country. Since the federal government's response was less than a well-oiled machine (more of a rickety, rusty, old-timey bicycle, a "bone shaker" with the really big front wheel), the states, counties, cities and neighborhoods stepped in with good and bad advice for slowing the spread of the disease, keeping the numbers (if the numbers are, in any way, real) in check so that fewer doctors and nurses died, keeping the health care system from getting overwhelmed, to give the virologists and other related white labcoat-wearing sciency folks time to develop a "cure" to a disease that's clearly manmade, much like the fear. Every country did its own thing, most of their own things being pretty damned Orwellian. Although the American response was haphazard, varying by the ideology of the regional leaders and general attitude toward science, toward fake science, toward whether or not they like Trump, toward collective and cooperative living and the ability to follow simple hand-washing directions, I, for one, was impressed by America's ability to adjust. Even with our ludicrous president (whose public health analysis and medical advice was, incredibly, more correct than the CDC's, though extremely unclear and mangled because the man's an idiot), we stepped up pretty well for a country full of people who think we're all still cowboys with metal horses and bigger guns.

…

Enough set-up. Anyway, Kelly and I met – at a decidedly less-than-"safe" distance, and talked. Not worried about catching any pretend disease, we just did our thing. Neither of us believes the government. So we were interrupted by customers getting takeout food at his half-window, and I'll spare you some of the conspiracy theorizing. (We both like to try and figure things out, so we both indulge in a healthy dose of conspiracy theorizing, but if you've read this far you should really know that by now. Also, when it turns out that the theorizers were right, can you even call it a theory?)

Kelly: "People look at it completely different."

Me: "Yeah, that's what gets to me about this, too. Some people think it's the beginning of the end of the human race. Other people think it's all 100% fake. I'm leaning toward fake. Something just doesn't smell right about it."

The highlights of the discussion were:

1) We get plagues about every one hundred years. One of Kelly's customers from earlier that day had told him about the bubonic plague in 1720, the cholera epidemic in 1820, and the Spanish Flu of 1919/1920. Now it's 2020. Apparently God works on a base-ten number system... and still throws really big tests our way... either that or opportunistic murderers are just really into round numbers. Still, we should've seen this coming. To quote our inspiration for this book, Bob Marley, "If you know your history/Then you will know where I'm coming from."

2) Read the back of your Lysol can. Kelly might be conspiracy minded, but he's not a slob, and he operates largely on common sense. Personal opinions aside, he was wiping his counter off after every time he, or anyone, touched it. He'd do this kind of cleaning anyway, but not as often, nor as rabidly. Sure, he knew this plague was over-hyped, but he also believes in customer service, even if the service the customer wants is massaging of their portion of mass hysteria. He was Lysoling his counter when he showed me the back of the Lysol spray can. Among the many other invisible pests Lysol can kill, it actually lists coronavirus. Giant worldwide Lysol conspiracy? The misunderstood Good Samaritans who make hand sanitizer having gotten so slowly and powerfully pissed off that they released a plague on the entire planet to get people to buy their little unfun alcohol products? The world may never know.

3) Kelly's getting predictably Apocalyptic. He veered into "Book of Revelation" and "Book of Jude" territory. Who couldn't see that one coming? This segued into what a bad idea it is to piss off China right now. They make pretty much everything everyone uses anywhere in the world. Maybe we should start directing our anger at a less influential country. Uganda? Maybe Belize. Yeah, screw those Belizian bastards. All our problems are clearly their fault.

Kelly said, "Right now The Father is so upset with what's going on in the world that He released this plague. No matter where you're from, Spain, Italy, wherever, He is displeased with us. It's time to get right with God."

I countered with, "OK, maybe, but I'm not sure if this thing's even real, much less a plague. It's too easy to lie at this moment, and there are too many people who are already terrified of something hazy, just waiting to find their next fear target."

4) Home remedies. *True Believer* had an appendix chapter about Kelly's grandparents' home remedies and how they are infinitely more effective than today's pharmaceuticals. The best, healthiest and most alcoholic of them is Kelly's Caribbean "Rum, lime and honey" cure for everything. It tastes better than antibiotics and has kind of the same effect. Think about it. Vitamin C and non-processed sugar indirectly from plants isn't all that different from things that even doctors admit will cure you. Kelly just wisely adds rum. Rum makes any medicine better. A spoonful of booze helps most anything go down…in the most delightful way.

5) Fear. Personally, I don't know how strong this virus is, if it's kind of real or not, or how it works, but I do know how strong fear is and how *that* works. It keeps people attentively slavish. It keeps people down, makes them hate themselves and covet what others have, mainly the others who don't have so much fear. Fear will kill you. I'm guessing we're about to experience a fear explosion the likes of which we've never seen before. [[I'm adding this part inside the brackets a year-and-a-half later, just to brag about being right that not only was there more real fear than I've ever seen, there was more fake fear. It was even crazier than I predicted, and I predicted near total insanity.]]

There's a segue between 5 and 6, and it kind of wrapped back to religion, ignorance, home remedies, Lysol AND the Apocalypse, tying this particular meeting into one neat, little ideological bow.

6) Running a Small Business During the Corona Outbreak. Kelly says, "I'm doing it. I'm adjusting to the reality of it, but I'm staying open and just serving to-go food through the little half window that came with the building. The main thing is it's still a lot like it was before, just changed a little. Word-of-mouth is still the best advertising."

7) Optimism/Belief. Any doctor dealing with any patient with a terminal illness will tell you how important a positive attitude is. Most doctors don't see hope, love and togetherness as the panacea it really is (Take two hopes and call me in the morning.), but those fuckers have been trained to think that they're demi-gods, and their superpower is dispensing the right pills, so it's not entirely their fault that they're incapable of looking at the world holistically. OK, it's mainly their fault, but patients seem to want them to act like they know what they're doing. Doctors are nothing more than professional guessers pretending to be professional knowers. At least carnival weight guessers admit they're trying to scam you.

It makes sense when you think about it. A belief in something larger than you and the short people you manufactured with your genitalia could be called faith, hope, and/or love. (The greatest of these is love, according to the Bible, but are they all just different words for the same phenomenon?) All three are linked. Belief and hope cause optimism, the love of humanity faithfully produces hope for humanity's future. Anything that comes your way, be it a curious, invisible man-made virus or a horde of marauding Mongol warriors, can best be dealt with if you have hope/faith/love. Talk to believers sometime, they're optimistic. Talk to people who love other people, they're optimistic. You can talk to pessimists, too, if you want, for the sake of comparison. There are plenty of them around. But my advice is to only talk to the pessimists once. Otherwise they will drag you down. Pessimism loves company.

TOPIC #19: APOCALYPTIC THOUGHTS

Since Kelly is already naturally a bit Apocalyptic in his thinking, things like the coronavirus "pandemic" are going to throw gasoline on an already-raging fire. They just are. That said, Kelly doesn't spend too much time worrying about disease. His home remedy of "lime, honey and a little Jamaican rum" really does work in most situations, and his faith sustains him. Adjust, keep the faith and keep moving forward.

Let's just deal with the current apocalyptic fuel, this particular pandemic. This day Kelly led off with, "There's so much out there about the coronavirus, so much that you don't know who to believe, what to believe." This is undeniably true. I've never seen a country so awash in conspiracy theory, in part because we currently have a president who pushes them (partly for his own financial and electoral advantage, but also because a lot of them are clearly real), in part because we've been lied to by our own government for so long, in such big ways, that conspiracy theory is inevitable. The combination of free speech + a federal government that won't admit even what we all kind of already know = conspiracy. Might as well theorize about it.

Kelly, with his Biblical worldview, is sustained by an actual faith. I am a believer down deep, but I don't have the kind of "wear-it-on-your-sleeve" comfort that many True Believers have. Unlike some of the more street-preachery purveyors of their faith, Kelly doesn't just spill it to everyone. He'll answer questions if you ask, but he's not directly pushing it, which is what makes him more successful at evangelizing than those who do.

That said, what I've always thought of as a sort of beautiful but childlike naiveté of the faithful is the tendency on some of their parts to WANT the world to end. Since I'm typing this at a moment in history that a lot of people think really might BE the beginning of the end of the world, ideas like this hit home. If the world ends, under this strain of Christian thought, doesn't that effectively consign billions of people to hell? "Get right with God." "There are no atheists in foxholes." Those kinds of sayings have a lot more power when you really do think the end is nigh.

...

Although the once-trusted, now clearly manipulative, medical purveyors of greed, lies and other related crap (aka The CDC), led by an evil genocidal midget who killed a bunch of gay guys in the 80's (possibly as a warm-up to this pretendemic), who's only really trusted at the moment because next to Donald Trump pretty much anyone seems reasonable, have advised us all not to leave our homes, neither Kelly nor I believe much of their propaganda, and so we both just upped our Vitamin C intake, vowed not to take whatever pretend "vaccine" they're fixing to launch our way, and went about our business, despite the growing chorus of groupthink telling everyone to label freethinkers like ourselves as enemies of humanity. We know you're lying, Dr. Fauci, we all know. Strange times, my friend, strange times indeed.

...

Naturally, our conversation turned to ideas like faith that day. In between serving walk-up customers jerk pork at his half window, Kelly and I discussed the end of the world. "It could be a plague sent by God to punish people."

That line, plus the picture of Bob Marley which was then sitting literally perched on Kelly's right shoulder, from my vantage point, led to talk of Babylon. Babylon was a real place, a place of exile for the ancient Jews, a place that has since come to mean exile in a strange land with poor morals. Is America the new Babylon? Bob said so, often. The Babylonian security forces were probably behind his assassination. They do like to kill the hopeful.

This led to the sort of schizophrenic way the rest of the world views America. The whole "land of opportunity" thing is still around, and it's still true. It's just contrasted with the lack of perceived soul in America. People come to America to make money, not to live for spiritually-fulfilling lives, ironic if you bring the Pilgrims into the equation.

It's the land of opportunity, but you still have to work for it. Despite the constant refrain of the hard-line conservatives bemoaning welfare queens or other things that don't really exist, or at least aren't as widespread as those guys think, America still has a pretty strong work ethic. We won't if we keep restricting foreigners from coming in. Who do you think does the actual work in this hardworking nation?

Kelly said on this fateful day, "When I came to the states, my entire concept of this country completely changed. There was a lot more freedom in Jamaica. We didn't have all the fancy stuff, the technology, but we were freer. It's like the radio. When I was a kid we didn't have TV or anything like that, but we had a radio. It was the country. I'm the son of a farmer, and the radio was a big thing. He had to hook the radio up to a car battery to get it to work, and everyone would gather around and listen. In America I had a radio in my taxi cab, but the authorities would be suspicious of a bunch of guys sitting around, listening to the radio."

I get it. In a country that repeats the idea that we are the land of freedom and opportunity roughly every five seconds, the idea that we may still have opportunity but we've lost the freedom still hasn't hit home enough for us to change that back. I think it will change back. We may not be free anymore, but we're still a rather defiant nation.

Don't be a follower. Followers are the people who actually listened to all the negativity. Listen to Kelly when he says, "If I followed people, I never would have reached this distance." Overcoming negativity is one of the standard hurdles on the path to success, and it helps with disease, too. I'm a big believer in the power of psychosomatism.

Shockingly, Kelly brought the conversation back to God's judgment. He thinks this is meant as a wake-up call to the planet. Maybe he's right – but I sure hope not.

TOPIC #20: FATE VERSUS FREE WILL
(and does God talk through people?)

This topic was probably inevitable in a philosophy book where one of the authors is a rabid Christian. It's been debated forever, long before there was such a thing as Christianity. The Greeks wanted the gods' favor too. The Egyptians wanted a fertile harvest and protection from their neighbors. Cavemen wanted to kill the mammoth who keeps eating their children.

To put this never-ending, probably unsolvable, conundrum in local Athenian context, Kelly was operating a Jamaican restaurant long before he settled into his Five Points location. I even visited the one on the edge of the perimeter on Milledge Avenue once, well before I knew Kelly. He had a Jamaican restaurant in Atlanta long before he'd even heard of Athens. His food has always been good, no matter the location, but Kelly's restaurant didn't really blossom until he moved into Five Points. It just fits. Drop by sometime, and you too will feel it.

The story of how he moved to that particular spot is all about free will versus fate. Before Kelly's was there, the building where he now has his restaurant housed a Steverino's (a sort of crappy sandwich shop). Kelly was operating his restaurant just a few miles away. He wanted a sandwich and a coffee for his commute home one night, and so he stopped into the neighboring Subway sandwich shop. (We'll skip over the fact that Subway is beyond terrible, and the fact that no one notices that their corporate slogan "Eat Fresh," if you take it at its word, is essentially telling people NOT to eat Subway.) As Kelly was ordering his food, the young black girl at the register pointed to the Steverino's next door and said, "That spot right there is going to be yours one day." Kelly responded with, "It's occupied." The girl doubled down. "I know it's going to be yours."

Kelly had noticed and craved the spot already – but that girl didn't know that. Steverino's wound up abandoning the spot a few months later, and Kelly scooped it up.

Was God talking through that girl that day? Kelly thinks so.

"Anything the Father has in mind for you, it's going to be hard for you not to get it."

Kelly had been in talks with a property owner to move to a different spot, one not nearly as central as the Steverino's, but something was holding him back. Fate? God's Plan? You tell me.

•••

Do you need more proof of the Hand of God in this decision? You do? OK. The Five Points spot has a half-window that Kelly has been using for To-Go orders during the "pandemic." The half-window had been sitting there, unused and largely unnoticed, for eleven years. Then 2020 hit, Kelly noticed it, cut through the thin layer of paint with a razorblade and has been using it ever since.

Kelly's philosophy on this is simple. "Back when I was living in Texas, I laid the foundation. I told the Father that I would put Him first and He told me He would take me where I needed to go. He's never turned His back on me since."

•••

Is the pandemic a TEST from God?

I won't take us too far down this philosophical rabbit hole, but when we discussed it, there was a Trump/Nebuchadnezzar analogy, a Covid/Seven Plagues of Egypt parallel and a few other comparisons that I'll admit seemed pretty convincing to me at the time, even though thinking about them later led me to think they weren't convincing at all.

How important is positive thinking?

Kelly and I agree on the importance of positive thinking. We both believe that our brains create our realities. I tend to get a little more New Agey on this one than Kelly, and he tends to go straight-up Biblical, but we arrive at roughly the same destination.

According to Kelly, "We all have negative thoughts. It just happens. The conscious mind says one thing and the subconscious mind says something else. The important thing is that you consciously push the negative thoughts out, you fight against them."

I can get onboard with that one.

…

End Times thinking?

When talking to a Biblical scholar like Kelly during a plague that, though exaggerated, is in actuality sickening old people the world over, it's hard for the conversation not to dip into Apocalyptic territory. I know we've discussed this topic already, but it keeps coming up, and Kelly and I are trying to give the recurring topics their due space in this book. Therefore, we did discuss Seven Seals, false prophets, whether Donald Trump really IS the anti-Christ and a few other things which we've already covered at least a little. (He's not. The anti-Christ doesn't need spray-tan.) I'll skip them for now, but they may come back up. I guess you'll have to wait and see.

TOPIC #21: DAWN DAVIS DROPS IN AS A SUBSTITUTE PHILOSOPHER FOR KELLY

It's a small world, after all. It's more than a little messed up that that deceptively simple truth is now pretty much only associated with Disney, ironically so, since Disney has now built theme parks on three continents and has bought up the rights to Star Wars AND Marvel Comics movie adaptations, and they're now truly down-sizing the childhood entertainment world by owning everything and have turned their bank vault into a really large, large world – but I digress. I digress before I've even started the damn chapter. This is going to be a problem.

...

I went over to Kelly's for one of our "regular" conversations. I ringed the word "regular" with quotation marks to make it ironic, since there's nothing regular about Kelly Codling, nothing regular about me, and definitely nothing "regular" about our far-ranging philosophical conversations. If they were "regular," they'd be boring, and we wouldn't have written this book. However, they are "regularly-scheduled," and purposefully timed for the generally-slow restaurant hours between standard lunch and dinner time on what is supposed to be a light day for restaurants, Tuesdays.

Usually these are the slow times at restaurants, the down time where the servers smooth their aprons and "wrap their silver," the chefs prep their food and yell at the servers, and the janitors are unshackled from their prison cells in the back room to clean up after the lunch crowd. But, this was a pandemic day, a Coronally-scheduled day. The "pandemic" has jiggled our schedules a lot, and since at the time of this writing, we're still not legally allowed to eat INSIDE of restaurants, lots of people are ordering to-go food from the eateries which have remained open, like Kelly's.

Therefore, when I arrived at his 5-Points location that Tuesday afternoon, I found a long line of hungry customers, a busy Kelbourne Codling and one woman I recognized sitting on Kelly's porch area/ outdoor picnic tables. I knew that I recognized her, but I couldn't quite place her. Normally, in situations like these, you fake your way through with the "Hey, great to see you, you. How are things? Wow, I can't believe we haven't seen each other in so long, my dear" trite sayings, to cover your lack of memory. But, since Kelly was busy, I was bored and she was sitting alone, I thought I'd try and figure out who this enthusiastic, skinny, artistic-looking woman was. It turns out that she was (and still is) a Christian film producer/writer/actress named Dawn Davis. She and her husband both proofread Kelly's and my first joint project, his biography, *True Believer*, six or so years back. As a publisher, I've worked with literally hundreds of proofreaders, but Dawn and her husband stand out in my memory. They were both really good, insightful, clearly fans of Kelly, his food, and, more importantly, his outlook on life. Their suggestions made me rethink some editorial decisions and generally made what was already a good book, great.

I appreciated their work, but since they were Kelly's friends, and, at the time about to move out of Athens for greener cinematic pastures, I didn't think I'd ever see them again, but there she was, just sitting in the center of one of the green middle-aisle picnic tables on Kelly's porch, quietly eating her jerk and occasionally working on something.

Kelly took a few quick work breaks and joined us for conversation, but mainly it was just Dawn and me that sunny Tuesday afternoon.

The talk, understandably, turned to the "pandemic." If you're reading this post-pandemic, then try and recall how often conversations in that time inevitably turned to Corona-talk. For a few months in the spring of 2020, it was damn near impossible for a conversation not to go COVID, at least for a few minutes.

Dawn makes what she calls "Cross-Cultural Positive" Christian movies. She's quick to point out that her message is less evangelistic than it is simply positive, showcasing how we've all got a lot more in common with each other than we think. As with most truly religious people, she's got a bit of glow to her, an undeniably happy aura. Kelly's got some of this too, but Kelly also has a quick temper and a wellspring of positively-released mild anger that fuels him, accompanying his inherent optimism. Both of these push him forward, and the optimism generally wins out over the anger, but the anger still lingers. And who could blame him for being a little angry? As his biographer, I know about all the nonsense he's had to confront and overcome since moving to America 50 years ago, some of it racial, some of it capitalistic, some of it domestic, and some of it just downright evil. More importantly, I know how Kelly's positivity has consistently defeated his anger, and wins more and more often as the calendar pages flip. My point here is – Kelly's got a bit of an edge, but Dawn Davis just has the happy glow of the securely spiritual.

"So many people are so paranoid these days. I just don't want to be around that."

Dawn's words echoed. If you lived through the early days of corona, you know how much loose, unfocused fear and paranoia was needlessly injected into an already-tense situation. Dawn made a good point. It's hard not to absorb what's around you, so in order to stay happy, it's best to surround yourself with happy people.

Dawn was not a pandemic denier. Neither was I (yet), nor Kelly for that matter. We were all skeptical about all of the nonsense that entangled and encircled the disease, but we all realized that there was actually a disease. A little skepticism is healthy. Too much is something else entirely. [[OK, this is another one of those "I'm adding this a while later" brackets. Now Kelly and I are now both pretty convinced the whole thing was planned. That doesn't make it less real, only less natural. Damn, I hate admitting that Trump was right, but he was. Also, the vaccines were totally pointless.]]

Dawn and I talked about how we both met Kelbourne Codling. She said, "I remember sitting down with Kelly when he ran his place on Milledge (Milledge Avenue, an Athens thoroughfare that once housed Kelly's budding Jamaican empire). I remember staring into his beautiful eyes. I remember his accent, his laugh. His is a good crazy."

Although I won't opine on the beauty of Kelly's eyes, I understood what Dawn was saying. Kelly's magnetism is hard to deny.

"He's an outside-the-box thinker. We need more of that."

I tried to be clever, pointing out that the phrase "outside the box" is now such an overused cliché that saying "outside the box" is ironically now "inside the box." Dawn is polite and gracious, so she didn't punch me in the face for derailing the conversation by trying to be clever. Thank you for that, Dawn.

As a True Believer herself, Dawn moved the conversation into the spiritual realm.

"A lot of people live in the Darkness. We (Kelly and Dawn and her husband) live in the Light. The Light will keep shining on us." Having a firm foundation of faith helps in tough moments.

Kelly's line of customers thinned out when a few of them realized that he wasn't serving ox-tail that day and left, to return another day, so he came out and joined us. These two believers turned the conversation to religious instruction, spiritual guides, evangelists, specifically televangelists. Unlike the two of them, I've always been skeptical of TV preachers. I have a hard time seeing past what appears to me to be a layer of hypocrisy, especially when they've made millions of dollars off of believers' donations, sent to them because they, theoretically, espouse the teachings of Jesus Christ, who said, "Blessed are you who are poor,/for yours is the kingdom of heaven," (Luke 6:20) and went on to say, "…But woe to you who are rich,/for you have already received your comfort." (Luke 6:24)

But that's me. Dawn and Kelly are both able to look past human hypocrisy and focus on the Divine Message itself. I should've asked them to promise to send me a postcard from heaven, since I might not wind up in the same Afterlife zip code.

Dawn mentioned how much she appreciated the preaching of T.D. Jakes. Kelly countered with Joel Osteen. I tried my damndest not to interject, but I couldn't help myself. I asked if Joel Osteen was one of those Gospel of Prosperity guys, as I'd heard. They said he wasn't. I'm still not convinced. (In case you don't know, the Gospel of Prosperity is the umbrella term for American Evangelical Protestant preaching that twists Jesus' message into its polar opposite, saying that Christ *wants* you to be rich, and conveniently ignoring the whole camel-eye-of-needle-rich-man-entering-heaven thing.)

They both defended Osteen and, since they knew a lot more about him than I do, I deferred, or to be more accurate, I shut up for a few minutes. Of course, I'm right on this one, but there's no need for me to mention that, except to say that I'm right, right, right, obviously, clearly right, righty, right, right, right-e-o, right.

The conversation easily turned to theology. These two amateur theologians cannot help themselves. (They haven't relinquished their amateur status and gone "pro," so they could still participate in the Olympics, if the Olympics ever adds sword drills. It could happen. They give out medals for Ping-Pong and Cross-country Skiing while shooting a Rifle, so it's not beyond the realm of possibility.)

Dawn and Kelly are both more theologically-minded than I, so I asked why it seems that so many sermons are so light on substance. A sadistic part of me, which in mentality is shockingly similar to the astonished questioners at the temple, hurling questions at the 12-year-old Christ, questions which he effortlessly deflected with wise answers, wanted to catch them in a net of hypocrisy. Kelly's a friend, and while I barely know Dawn, she seems like a gracious, kind, honest soul, and I know she's a hell of a copyeditor, but still, I felt like trying to poke some holes that day. Like the questioners at the temple during Passover, I was proven wrong and small by their abiding faith and enduring wisdom.

"Why are so many sermons so thin, so lacking in theology?" I asked.

"Sometimes when you're down in the Pit, you can't hear complex theology. If you listen harder, it'll make sense," Dawn answered.

I started to respond with something snarky, but I caught myself when I realized they were politely telling me to open my mind. Damn it, they just put me in my place. I don't like admitting this, but it IS necessary from time to time.

Dawn and Kelly both prefer their faith to the facemasks and rubber gloves the news is telling us to wear all the time now. They both mentioned the often insidious effects of peer pressure. Peer pressure doesn't stop when you graduate high school. In fact, usually it grows and grows, metastasizing until we can't even recognize it as peer pressure anymore.

"Getting people to wear masks and gloves all the time outside actually breaks down the immune system," I added. They both agreed that constantly testing the immune system is the only way to strengthen it. I wholeheartedly agreed. In other words, by advising us to wear masks, they extended the strength and the length of the problem. (In retrospect, this conversation was probably what set Kelly and me off into looking into the reality of this clearly planned, obviously planned, I-can't-believe-everyone-doesn't-see-how-obviously-it-was-planned "pandemic.") [[Oh, here's future Bowen, adding that, a few years later, even the CDC and others who TOLD us to wear the masks, admitted that they were pointless. Point to Bowen and Kelly.]]

That said, all three conversers on Kelly's porch that day also agreed that, while we may disagree with the prevailing "wisdom" of the day, as reported by the fear-mongering news outlets, doing at least some of what they advise in order to quell other peoples' fears is, nonetheless, valuable to society. In other words, none of us were about to grab an AK-47 and start protesting state stay-at-home orders any time soon, but wearing a mask on occasion is something we all three do even though we know it's pointless. Living anywhere that isn't a cave on a mountaintop requires that you sometimes do stupid stuff you completely disagree with.

When one of us mentioned the news, a favored topic of Kelly's and mine, Kelly said yet another simple yet undeniably true statements for which he is famous, "I don't get my news from the TV. I get it from people."

Makes sense.
I trust people I know.
I don't know the corporate presidents of news stations.
Therefore, I trust people, not the news.
Take that lesson to heart.

TOPIC #21-1/2: PROPHESY, THE AMERICAN WAY

This is a continuation of the same discussion. Dawn stuck around. I stuck around. But, after Kelly went back to serve a few more to-go customers, he returned to hold court. Dawn and I sat in mild awe at this point since Kelly is really good at holding court.

Kelly launched back into one of his standards – The Book of Revelation. This pandemic has really brought out the raging Apocalyptic street preacher in Kelly Codling.

Since Kelly keeps coming back to it, I thought I might should actually sit down and read the Book of Revelations. The first thing I noticed was that there is no "S." It's not the Book of Revelations, plural. It's just one long, action-packed Revelation. One book. One revelation. The second thing I noticed was how much it reads like a Hollywood action movie script: an angry red dragon chasing a woman who's just given birth and who narrowly escapes from the swooping dragon on wings prepared for her, by God, to a safe place in the desert, a beast rising from the sea and wreaking havoc, then another beast, this one from the Earth. That second beast turns out to be the Antichrist I've heard so much about. He's like the first beast's Vice-President, in a very Dick Cheney kind of way, ruling while saying he's subservient, forcing everyone to get his permission to buy or sell anything, and, of course, marking everyone on the hand or forehead with his special number, 666.

Isn't Trump Tower's Manhattan street address #666? I'm just asking. For the record, I don't think Donald Trump is the Antichrist. The

Antichrist seems a lot smarter and is able to hide his rage a little better. Also, the Antichrist has better hair.

I'm not saying that Trump's not evil. He's clearly evil, just not Biblically evil.

Segueing off Revelation slightly, Kelly talked about a film he watched in college in Washington, D.C., in the 1970's called "Future Shock" (based on the book of the same name written by Alvin Toffler). This black-and-white, reel-to-reel film predicted pagers before anyone knew what that was, predicted the death of pay phones when no could imagine a world without them, predicted that many large businesses were going to merge, that we'd all be tracked through our telephones before anyone could conceive of such a communication device being able to fit into a pocket. Looking back, it seems like a really prophetic piece of literary cinema.

Since Kelly watched this as a class assignment, later, when the teacher assigned a paper to be written on any topic, Kelly wrote an essay about "Future Shock." When the papers were graded and handed back to the class, the teacher called Kelly into his office after class, and asked, "Kelbourne, where did you get all this information?"

"From the film you made us watch."

The teacher thought for a moment, and then assigned Kelly the longest homework deadline in academic history, "30 or 40 years from now, look back on this."

And he has…

TOPIC #22: IF YOU HEAR THE PEOPLE, YOU DON'T NEED TO FEAR THE PEOPLE

Since our last meeting, there was yet another prominent American police murder of an unarmed black man. It's nothing new. What is new is the preponderance of cell phone cameras. What is new is the economic effect of a worldwide pandemic. (Even if it's clearly half-fake, the results are still the same.) What is new is the people having time on their hands because they lost their job due to the "pandemic," corporations not even pretending to hide the fact that they don't at all care about their employees anymore, a president who clearly hates brown people and doesn't understand the concept of empathy, AND the generalized sense of fear and uncertainty of the year 2020.

In case you just woke up from a coma and the first thing you're doing is reading this book, first off, let me say "Good call." Second, allow me to set the scene:

In May of the year 2020 George Floyd, a middle-age black man in Minneapolis, Minnesota, is arrested for using a counterfeit 20 dollar bill at a local business establishment. The cops come, detain him in typically violent fashion. This time, however, one particular cop, who is – surprise, surprise – an angry, scared white man, after already hav-ing secured Mister Floyd's hands behind his back, with George's face planted against the lute-warm, Minnesota asphalt, feels the need to also shove his knee into Floyd's neck, kneeling on him roughly. Floyd tells the cop that he can't breathe. Three other cops stand around, not seeming to notice that their co-worker is currently in the middle of murdering a dude. In fact, the murderer and his angry colleagues are more concerned with keeping bystanders away from their revenge fantasy than about anything having to do with the mysterious concept of "justice" (whatever that is). One of the bystanders tells the kneeling, uniformed coward that he's killing George Floyd. Another films the entire episode, all eight minutes and change of murder-kneeling. George Floyd dies – right there on the street. The video goes out to the world, goes "viral," and all hell breaks loose in the most predictably unpredictable kind of way.

What follows is a wave of half-peaceful, half-riotous, protests all around the country, and a little in England too, since England's now, ironically, kind of America's bitch, our vassal state. The protests are intense, mainly peaceful, but there is some looting and property damage, not much, relatively-speaking, considering the size and scope of the protests, but actual looting, and definitely enough to justify an intense response in the minds of those who were looking to be justified. The people are fed up with police brutality and Institutional Racism. Black America has reached a breaking point. This scares the living feces out of "President" Trump and any white people whose deepest fears tend to drift toward the young-black-guy-with-dreadlocks-banging-their-daughters variety. Since a LOT of those kinds of guys occupy high "elected" office, in response to the protests, the states and cities and federal government send out thousands of riot-gear-clad, empathy-lacking, meathead fascists in matching outfits. Was that descriptor too fanciful?

The police, the National Guard, even members of other stray other federal agencies (but, sadly, not the EPA, or anyone from the Office of Weights and Measures –would've been funnier) get sent out, too. All of those guys are heavily-armed. Many of them were already angry, and already also didn't seem to like black people, and, since they already were the cousins of the very brutalizers whose aggression set off the protests to begin with, but they're still too scared of black people to ever change, these guys got brutal. They beat up pretty much anyone in their way, including the elderly, the clergy, the hippie, and some journalists who were standing in front of the guy they wanted to beat the shit out of. The people got mad. The brutalizers stayed just as brutal. The people got madder. A decent amount of property destruction and some mild looting happened, though still, considering their size and scope, it was mainly peaceful. And so it went. This long-overdue eruption of righteous anger made American protests cool again, because even some of the white people who are really scared of black people kind of, on some level, wish they themselves were black, joined the marches. It's a weird, but interesting, psychological phenomenon. And this time, many faux-aggrieved white people marched with the understandably-aggrieved black people

Any single other president would try and calm the nation, but not this one. In the middle of this, "President" Trump got scared (because he's one of those guys who is clearly just really afraid of black people) and retreated to his secret bunker until it occurred to him that hiding from a bunch of hippies might tarnish the pretend "tough guy" image he's adopted to get try and get re-elected. So then he acted, in the only way he knows how…stupidly. Trump tear-gassed a bunch of protesters outside of the White House, some of whom were clergy, in order to walk across the street and have an obviously staged photo-op in front of a church, which didn't want him there, where he held a Bible (upside down) and pretended, once again, to be Christian. Since a lot of the crowd was live-tweeting or in some other way recording the event, the world noticed. This did nothing to quell the protests.

The policeman/murderer was arrested. The protests continued. Eventually the policeman's three buddies were arrested. As I'm typing this, the protests have not stopped. Some of the more outside-the-box thinkers among the protesters want to, in their words, "Defund the Police," to scrap these well-armed, poorly-dressed, polyester-clad gangs altogether and start over. It's an idea worth considering.

It's also a slogan that the regressive elements, the same guys who are terrified of black people, have latched on to, as a thin excuse for their not supporting America's finally living up to our beautiful founding ideals.

There has been some violence, some looting, some setting of police cars on fire, one setting of a police station on fire, and the inevitable result of this, curfews set in major American cities. While the overwhelming majority of the protests are non-violent (if you take the police out of the equation), there has been some violence. Naturally, this is what conservative media is focusing on, though less than they normally do. Naturally, a certain segment of the population of scared white people in power are talking in some of their favorite coded language about "law and order," "taking back the streets," or whatever cliché, overused jargon they toss out in times like these. That said, this protest feels different than those which came before, and I've lived through a lot of police killings and their resulting protests. This one feels like it's sticking. The protesters come in all shapes, ages, sizes, and most importantly, all colors. There are plenty of white people. This one's gonna stick.

OK, so that was a really long set-up. I get it. Except for you, newly-awakened-from-your-decade-long-slumber Coma Guy, everyone else reading this lived through these events. Hell, since you're future people, you know more about it all than I do. Freaking future people.

That was, indeed, a really long set-up, but I feel it was necessary. First of all, Kelly and I did have a philosophy session this day, but it was less verbal than most. We tried to do our normal thing, but protest was in the air and on TV. We both kept sneaking sidelong glances at CNN until we just went silent and stared at the human drama in all its glory, with the overflowing hope for a better, less murdery, tomorrow spilling out into everyone watching. Watching these protests, I'm proud of America. I was worried that we'd forgotten how to protest, and passionate dissent is so central to a functioning liberal democracy that its lack is either due to complacency, largesse, or, more likely, an overpowering government that pretends like it's not overpowering us.

Damn, that was almost four full pages worth of set-up. We haven't even gotten to the philosophy yet.

Kelly and I started to talk about something else, but we both just rambled a little for a while, half-watching the TV, as the word-to-si-

lence ratio went from one extreme slowly to the other. I won't record
the stuff we were going to talk about, but I will relate a little of what
we DID talk about.

Kelly: "People are tired of the abuse, the racism, being treated like
they're nothing."
Me: "Clearly."
Kelly: "It's like Exodus. Babylon."

He trailed off for a few minutes. I'm not sure if I really get the parallel to the second book of the Bible here. American black people and
ancient Jews in Egypt were both highly mistreated. They were both
thought of as second-class citizens, both slaves in every sense. Also,
both groups were thought of as being a little mysterious, curious, not
fully human like the ruling class, strange but interesting.

Me: "This protest is really going to do something, change something. What? I don't know, but something."
Kelly: "Powerful people are scared by numbers like that. They love
their population control, but people will only put up with being slaves
to oppression for so long."
Me: "Something really IS going to come from this. Look at all the
white people in the crowd."
Kelly: "Unless Trump declares Martial Law and cancels the election, he's going to lose." [[Once again, my co-author, Kelly, proves
himself the Nostradamus of North Georgia.]]
Me: "Oh, I know. But if he did declare Martial Law America
would burn, I mean, just burn to the ground. I don't think even he's
that stupid."
Kelly: "All he knows how to do is pit people against each other."

The news focused in on a protest outside a Los Angeles police station. There were thousands of peaceful, but determined, people outside
of that one police station.

Kelly: "Why doesn't someone just come out? Some official?"

Me: "Yeah, they could break up the crowd if they'd just come out and listen. It seems like it'd be so easy."

Kelly: "This is bigger than COVID."

Me: "This is bigger than racism."

Kelly: "This is bigger than anything I've seen in years."

Me (tearing up a little): "I'm just so damn proud of America right now."

TOPIC #23: PRETTY MUCH JUST A CONTINUATION OF LAST SESSION'S TOPIC
(but with the added benefit of hindsight from a few weeks of collected wisdom)

FEAR.

FEAR.

EVERYONE BE AFRAID, BE VERY AFRAID.

Once again, due to the importance of "current" national events, Kelly and I had a Session with CNN on in the background. The "pandemic" and the anti-police brutality protests that sprang up after America saw the video of a white Minneapolis cop murdering George Floyd ARE the news these days.

If I'm being optimistic, I think that these protests could launch a New Age, the Age of Aquarius, a more tolerant era, a epoch where we care more for the well-being of other humans than we do about hoarding money and stuff and clinging to social class structures that no longer make any sense, a time of equality, where race isn't our biggest dividing line, an age of decreasing state power, where the officials in charge of public safety aren't making 50 percent of the people they're supposedly protecting feel like crapping their pants every time they see one of these "protectors and servers."

If I'm being pessimistic, this is just another protest, to which our leaders will pay lip service but then turn around and do nothing, with no resulting real, systemic reform. Those in power tend to say one thing but do the opposite. If we pay closer attention to their bullshit, they might at least slow it down a little.

But I'm an optimist by nature. So is Kelly.

Kelly: "They're not going to put the fear in me."

That says it all. Don't let them scare you. They're trying to scare you. It's what they *do*. It's an effective way to control you – but it doesn't have to be. Trust me, if you stop being so scared, they'll switch tactics. They don't care if you're afraid, just that you stay in your place and don't rock the boat. Their most effective means of achieving this has traditionally been spreading fear. But, and here's the rub, if you simply stop being afraid, they'll stop trying so damn hard to scare you. It's on you…and me…and all of us, to make this change. Once we do, we'll discover that 99 percent of the nonsense they said to scare us and keep us in our place was, of course, utter nonsense. Check out the DSM some time (Diagnostic and Statistical Manual – the psychiatrists' Bible), and look at all the stuff they now call "disorders." It's insane how many different ways they've come up with to label us "insane."

...

Later we turned the discussion back to the pandemic for a bit. Both Kelly and I are, to say the least, skeptical of the Official Story. I know it's real. Two people I know and care about have had it. They've also both fully recovered. I don't know one single person who's died from it. Personally, I doubt the numbers, the statistics, pretty much every-thing they say on TV about it. By now, everyone other than a small portion of the, recently-emboldened, right-wing fringe movement agrees that it is a real virus. But that's about the spot where everyone stops agreeing.

Kelly harps on the recycled carbon that comes about from wearing masks all day, every day. I agree with his logic, but I'm not as adamant on this point as he is.

I try and bring up the fact that we're an extremely unhealthy nation, and maybe that factors into why we have so many more deaths from this disease than other countries, assuming the numbers are at least somewhat real. [[They're not.]] We eat like crap. Hell, sometimes we care so little about what's in our food that we probably are eating actual crap. That leads me to one positive conclusion from this virus — people are eating a little better. People are planting gardens outside of their homes. We never should've stopped growing our own food. We did. But we shouldn't have. Now we are growing a little again. That's a positive.

Kelly: "We don't know what to believe. Trump? Dr. Fauci? The CDC? The WHO?"

Much like Kelly, I trust other live human beings considerably more than the TV or the internet. Therefore, both Kelly and I like to take little, unofficial surveys of people we meet about topics we're unsure of. Try it some time, it's way more honest than the news. So, since both of us are skeptical of this virus, or at least of the tangential information coming at us hard and fast and all-day about this virus, we've both conducted some amateur local polling.

Kelly: "About 2 to 3 percent of people say the virus is not real. About 5 to 10 percent of people think it's real, but it's not as serious as they're saying. The rest are just going along with the news."

Me: "That sounds about right, but I think the percentage of people who doubt the seriousness is larger than 10 percent. Maybe close to 25 percent. Hard to tell, since some of them aren't being very vocal about it."

Kelly: "One thing I've noticed. Women are way more scared of it than men. I had a couple come in the other day, a husband and wife, both doctors, and the wife wore the mask, and the husband had one but wasn't wearing it. She said, 'You should wear a mask because I care about you,' to him."

Me: "Yeah, you're right about the gender divide. Some of that is that men don't like being told what to do, and women are just simply a lot more scared of invisible stuff than men. Also, women tend to trust doctors more than men."

Kelly agreed. Though, since both of us naturally distrust doctors to an alarming degree, we're probably not the best control group for this particular amateur local poll.

...

RANDOM QUESTIONS THAT CAME AS A RESULT OF THIS SESSION:

"If we can talk to each other as easily as we now can, how come we have such a hard time communicating with each other?"

"A lot of people don't have very broad horizons."

"I'm terrified that they're going to use this virus as a way of getting rid of small businesses." (Kelly, asking an especially important question for the two of us, since we both run small businesses. That said, both of our businesses, his restaurant and my publishing house, are doing okay in this period. People still want spicy food, and now we all have time enough on our hands to finally write the book we've been meaning to for years.)

...

AND THE STRANGEST PART OF THIS SESSION:

Kelly's big on predictions. He likes *The Book of Revelation*, medieval prophets, and Middle Age prognosticators, and refers back to that book/movie/film strip "Future Shock" often. Personally, I prefer *The Farmer's Almanac*. It's a more expansive book of predictions than you'd think.

Anyway, as an aside from our dual-topic pandemic/protests discussion, Kelly randomly ventured into tin foil hat territory, relating a story from his days living in Texas.

"I've lived 51 years in the USA. In Texas I remember people talking about people being micro-chipped. I was in an Albertson's (regional grocery store), and a gentleman was walking out one day and instead of paying he just swiped his hand over the register and paid for his groceries. I watched him do it. So, I was curious. I went up to the manager and asked him about the chip. He got mad and kicked me out of the store. That's when I knew I was right. I told my daughter about it when it happened. She pooh-poohed the idea then, but four years ago, she came back and said, 'Daddy, you were right.'"

...

Even I am skeptical of this story. I trust Kelly like I trust few other people to whom I'm not genetically-linked, but still, this one is a stretch even for me. It's probably true. I've never known Kelly to lie. In fact, if anything, he's too honest. It gets him in trouble…or rather, it would get him in trouble all the time if he weren't smiling when he said things. Look at pictures of Kelly from years ago. He looks much angrier man than he does now. According to the man himself, he was. But his determination to reach his goals, his abiding faith in The Father, as he calls Him, and his love of humanity turned the anger around. If he can do that, so can you, so can I, so can everyone.

TOPIC #24: A GRABBAG OF RANDOMNESS

As the "pandemic" raged on, with all of its strangeness, as the protests against police brutality continued and continued to be demonized, Kelly and I continued to meet. This meeting was all over the place. Sometimes we managed to stick to one topic, sort of, but other days the conversation was all over the place.

1) National Coin Shortage?

Lately I've seen stores with a warning that goes something like, "Due to the national coin shortage, we will be stealing some more of your money. This time it's coins." Maybe there really is a national coin shortage, or maybe this is one of the many ways the powers that be are trying to eliminate cash from our society – in order to track us even more. Credit cards are trackable. Cash ain't.

Kelly and I agree that we need to keep cash as a part of the monetary system. Cash is better than credit. Credit is a nothing. Cash is at least tangible. When you drill down a little, all currency is truly a nothing, but at least you can see cash, you can smell it. You could taste it, but I wouldn't.

Anyway, we're both skeptical of this supposed national coin shortage. It might be real, but lizard people might be real too.

2) Teaching Methodology

Kelly: "Why don't they just do school outside?"

Me: "Yes. That solves the problem, doesn't it? Half the parents won't send their kids anyway."

Kelly: "Then they wouldn't have to worry about masks and nose tests and all that."

Me: "I'm with you, but you know this is too good and too obvious a solution for them to ever actually do it, right?"

Kelly: "So sad."

3) *Pangerdemic*

Kelly: "Everybody's too mad."

Me: "I don't think they even know why."

Kelly: "Corona is getting to them. They don't even know which direction to turn."

Me: "Trump doesn't help."

Kelly: "He never does."

4) New World Order

This is one of the conspiracy theorists' favorite phrases. Is it a Freemason/Illuminati thing? Is it just something a stray currency designer, in a fit of whimsy, tossed onto the dollar bill? A once-positive phrase slowly turned ominous? Or is it not at all a conspiracy theory and merely representative of the inescapable but harmless fact that a lot of our Founding Fathers were Freemasons?

As this phrase pertains to the coronavirus, it has taken on an even darker connotation. I didn't think it could get any darker, but it has. These days the theorists and other skeptical thinkers believe it represents the ways we're being conditioned by current ideas/mandates/ etc. Are we being conditioned to wear masks (ostensibly as protection – but really as a control device)? Are we being loosened up to the idea that old people are supposed to die when they pass a certain age? (If so, my guess is it's the age when the state feels the oldies can no longer make money for the elites, which is when? 65?) Is this another excuse to try and get us to stop using cash money, so everything we do can be traced and tracked? Is "contact tracing" just another excuse to spy on us all the time? Have my random questions started to veer off the track I originally intended here? (The last question has an obvious answer. The others – not so much.)

Personally, I think it's about 50/50. Kelly is even more skeptical than I am about the public health now. I think it's because Jamaica has been sane about the masks and the social distancing, and they haven't had much pandemic death at all. America, of course, politicized it, and we're dying by the truckload…or so they say. If this thing's real, we would naturally be the country with the most death. We love nothing more than being #1. We're not very good at doing what we're told. Bear in mind that this a country formed by other countries' rejects, all of whom had problems with authority and a violent desire to destroy something. It's ironic how controlled a society we are now.

•••

The medical aspect of this thing is so freaking bizarre. Many non-American doctors have been curing this thing in ten seconds with quinine (well, what is essentially quinine)…if you believe a certain segment of journalists.

No one has been cured period…if you believe the other segment of journalists.

This is the worst thing to ever happen to mankind.

This is an exaggerated flu.

Be afraid. Be very afraid.

Eeenngh, be a little cautious maybe, but never fear, and "Don't worry 'bout a thing/'cause every little thing's gonna be all right."

•••

People can be easily frightened. America ranks at the top of the list for countries that promote fear of total idiocy. In my life I've seen promotional campaigns warning us to be afraid of:

» meat AND tofu

» sex AND abstinence

» war AND peace

» spanking your kids AND not spanking your kids

You get the idea. If FDR was right, and the only thing we have to fear is fear itself, then none of it, no disease, no natural disaster, no pandemic, actually merits fear. Caution, sure. Fear, no. Caution is common sense. Fear is paralyzing.

Almost all the women I know are terrified of this coronavirus. About 1/3 of the men are, too. Whether we should be afraid of this thing or not, we clearly are. What's not being reported by the "news" outlets is the simple breakdown of men versus women. Simply put, women are more wary of disease than men. Underneath, that's probably about babies, which makes sense. When you factor the unconscious human actions on behalf of the next generation into gender discussions, they make a lot more sense. Of course, we don't do that, but then again, common sense isn't all that common these days.

5) Good News

As with all phenomena, there is always a silver lining. Even a global pandemic can have positive outcomes, intended or not. We are growing more food outside of our own homes now. That's good. We never should have stopped.

The specter of death (no matter how real) causes us to appreciate our loved ones more. That's good. We always should.

We're spending more time outside. Vitamin D is good stuff.

We're doing things we've put off for years.

We're calling people we haven't spoken to in decades, just to see if they're still alive. Yeah, it's a bit morbid, but still good.

We're seeing things that, in our normal constant everyday rush, we haven't seen. The biggest example is that now white people can see the police in the way that black people always have. It's not the only example. We see that disasters, natural or man-made, are different experiences for rich people than they are for poor people. We see pollution and how easy it is to stop it. We see our neighbors as fellow travelers on this roller coaster called Life.

All this seeing won't necessarily translate into action, but it's a good first step.

6) Politics

Yeah, Kelly and I talk about politics too much, no doubt. But even the most repeated, rehashed argument or discussion topic can occasionally lead to something new. I'm pretty sure this is a version of an old quotation, but in this meeting, when the discussion inevitably turned political, Kelly, as he is wont to do, neatly summarized it all, saying, "Politics is the art of making people feel good while robbing them."

Brilliant, no?

7) Kelly's Home Remedy for Everything

I know we've written this one in this very book a few times now, but it's such good advice that it bears repeating.

Local honey, lemon/lime juice and Jamaican rum cures pretty much everything.

TOPIC #25: LIKE PULLING TEETH

For all of you wee folk, you little youngish people, you unformed i-generation moron kiddies, there once was a common fill-in-the-blank expression that clearly originated in a time when there weren't many dentists. "__________ is like pulling teeth."

You see, wee people, pulling teeth used to be difficult. If there's no laughing gas and no sadistic guy who failed out of medical school peering into your mouth involved, then it's just not an easy thing to pull your own teeth. Look it up. People used to take a few shots of whiskey, tie one end of a string around a rotting tooth and the other end around a doorknob, gird themselves for the inevitable pain, and then slam the door. If the person was positioned right, and preferably had a few friends to hold him back, then the tooth came out, the pain flashed and then slowly subsided, and eventually the man went about his business, minus one tooth. Pulling your own teeth was hard, not impossible, but hard.

Expressions tend to last a few generations beyond when they made total sense, because kids pick up expressions from their parents, who picked them up from their parents. So, even though Kelly and I both grew up in a time when dentists abounded, we both knew the expression.

This was my long-winded, semi-historical way of setting up the conditions for this day's conversation. Kelly was wiped out today. His eyes were doing that long-haul trucker thing, that high school student who stayed up all night last night cramming for a first-period math test, took it, and is currently trying to stay awake in sixth period Social Studies class thing.

It had been a long week for Kelly. For me too, but it's easier to set your own schedule when you're a book publisher than when you run a restaurant. Since this pandemic has been rough on small businesses, and since Kelly has to be open when people want to pick up food, he can't set as many of his own hours as I can.

It wasn't our best discussion. It was barely a discussion at all. But even being half-comatose can't keep a natural philosopher like Kelly from philosophizing, so there was some discussion.

...

Politics dominated the news in the time between our previous meeting and this one. It's a presidential election year and both the Democratic and Republican National Conventions had just concluded, so the political frenzy that accompanies the emotional side of American politicking was running high.

Political conventions are interesting pageantry, but if you think about it, they don't really mean anything. Even the behind-the-scenes wrangling of "platform committees," the only real drama involved in non-brokered conventions, are largely pointless. They're just four day commercials on behalf of the grandeur of two egocentric people.

This year, thanks to the "pandemic," a lot more of it was done remotely, via computer-based communication. The Democrats' was all virtual. The Republicans' was partly virtual, but since our current president is a showman, a deranged narcissist, and has an unquenchable desire for a daily reminder that people love him, he did manage to arrange a fireworks show that spelled out his name in bright colors in the sky. I'll admit that it was a pretty good show. However, since I can't imagine anyone who hasn't already made up his mind about who he's going to vote for this go-round, it was all still mainly just pageantry. The Democrats wanted to show what national unity might look like, and the Republicans wanted to show fealty to their dear leader. And they both did that, kind of.

Emotion is always high in American politics, but this year it's higher than I've ever seen. Except for the time before, during and right after the Civil War, I can't imagine that it's ever been this high. What's frightening is that many of the issues being discussed today are the same ones discussed during the Civil War: race relations, the proper role of the federal government, the economy and the always-popular American political hobby of searching for traitors.

Since even though Kelly is maybe the best conversationalist I've ever met, he still can't debate while sleeping, I'm going to skip laying out most of what we talked about that day, in favor of a recent personal example of the nonsense level of emotion about the 2020 presidential election.

...

Once a year I have a reunion with my high school friends. It's a great tradition. Everyone should do it. We go to different vacation spots, catch up, play poker, make fun of each other, drink too much, play golf, and make fun of each other some more. True male bonding involves a decent amount of ripping on each other. It's great. It keeps you humble. And old friends have far more ammunition for jokes than anyone other than your mother (And presumably your mother isn't always making fun of you, at least I hope not. If she is, find a new mother.).

One of my best friends is an OB-GYN in rural Alabama. In the last few decades he's taken a hard right turn politically. He's a huge fan of Donald Trump. He obsessively listens to right-wing radio hosts. He knows that I'm an independent and he keeps trying to get me to join his cult, I mean his side. Part of our yearly ritual, since we're the only two members of the crew who don't live around the greater Atlanta area, is to meet up at one of our Atlanta friends' houses, get in one car and head out. We always talk politics. Something I've always respected about my nameless doctor friend is that he and I are able to politely debate, to disagree with each other without anger, without thinking that the other person is somehow suspect, or mildly traitorous. This year's drive was a little more emotional.

It wasn't a shouting match. We're old friends. I value friendship more than political allegiance. In normal times, he does, too. But I had to control his emotions twice in this year's six-hour discussion. Both times followed the same pattern, a pattern I imagine is playing itself out all across the amber waves of grain.

We'd pick a topic, then he'd lay out his vision, his reasoning behind his opinions, and then he'd ask some semi-Socratic questions about what I believe. Even though some of this is territory we'd covered in earlier years, since there's a year between these talks, it still requires an update, which is fine, which we both enjoy. But the emotion behind this year's rants looked like a reverse right triangle. He'd start talking, then the talk would slowly begin to form a rant, then his emotions would start to come out, then he'd ask a question, then, unsatisfied with my answer, the emotion would grow.

He's one of the best friends I'll ever have, so I know how to defuse his emotion. It's easy. I just make a joke. It doesn't even have to be a good joke. As long as I make a joke, he realizes that he's getting emotional, and then the anger flattens, and we change the subject. This happened twice on this ride. I almost needed to make a third joke, but by then he'd recognized the pattern and self-regulated.

What amazed me was that this was new. There was never this level of emotion. Both "sides" in this election think that the very future of the country depends entirely on the outcome, and they're more than willing to shout that to their people. There's always a little of this with American presidential elections, but this year's emotion level is through the freaking roof.

What frightens me most right now is, what if my friend was right?

...

OK, I promised you some Kelly in this chapter. You probably bought this book because you like Kelly, you're curious about Kelly's philosophy on life, you're on some level jealous of the Kellyness of Kelly (I get it, I am a little, too.), you simply wish you were born in a country as cool and universally-beloved as Jamaica, you like to think about the big issues of life, or maybe you just forgot to buy your wife a Christmas present, and you happened to be at Kelly's on December 23rd. I don't know why you bought this book, but I'm glad you did.

Let's list today's discussion topics as Word Jumbles:

1 – (one word) C, T, E, A, N, Y, R, I, U, N, T

2 – (two words) S, E, F, A, L   &   O, T, H, P, E, P, R

3 – (one word) R, H, T, U, T

Now let's waste some paper and list the answers to today's topic Word Jumbles on the following page. Don't cheat.

Did you cheat? Why? There's no one looking. If you cheat at solitaire, then you'll cheat at paying taxes, at paying employees, and at predictable Word Jumbles in rant-heavy philosophy books. If you cheated, you're a terrible human being, a worthless waste of space. I will defecate on your grave, often and preferably with diarrhea. Still, I promised you some answers, and answers you shall receive:

1 – UNCERTAINTY

2 – FALSE PROPHET

3 – TRUTH

If I had to pick three words to come out of what was far and away our worst discussion to date, those would be the three. They were applied to American politics, to the ongoing "pandemic," to the mood on the streets as it pertains to the ongoing protests about police brutality, racism, and state power, and to what both of our respective small businesses might look like in a month.

The world at this moment in time is overflowing with Uncertainty, with False Prophets, and with Truth. All three of them share one thing. They all hurt. They're all everywhere. It's not always easy to know which is which, but all three of those are definitely floating around in the ether.

TOPIC #26: ORIGAMI: THE UNHERALDED CONSPIRACY THEORY

Kelly and I met inside his restaurant on a Friday afternoon. It was surprisingly not busy at his restaurant that day, which was odd, but did give us more time to talk.

We had a sporadic conversation that Friday, with plenty of interruptions, because even when Kelly's not busy he still has a pretty steady stream of hungry customers. Therefore, I'll just give you the highlights:

...

A SMALL GESTURE GOES A LONG WAY

I was staring out onto Kelly's front porch of his Five Points restaurant, thinking about how lucky he was to have an outdoor eating space for this pandemic. People can take their food home, but they can also sit outside and eat, not be totally shamed by the Angry Mask Contingent. Kelly has a little thatch wall hanging which, along with his choice of standard Jamaican color scheme, turns his porch into a little slice of the Caribbean quite effectively. The porch predates Kelly's restaurant, but all he did was repaint it and hang one thing on the wall and BAM, it's Jamaica. A little goes a long way.

...

WATCH YOUR TONGUE

As we've said, everyone's angry. Everyone's on edge. Everyone's waiting to explode, looking for the spark to ignite their internal flame-thrower.

Kelly: "These days if you say the wrong word to the wrong person, you're gonna hear about it."

Me: "More so than before this pandemic."

Kelly: "A lot more."

...

WHAT IS TRUTH?

A lot has been written about this era. It's been called a "Post Truth" epoch. I hate that distinction for multiple reasons. First off, it presupposes that truth will never come back. Second, it claims that there is no truth now. The reality is there's a hell of a lot of propaganda right now, but that doesn't mean the truth isn't hidden in plain sight, like it usually is. Truth is not something that could ever be totally stamped out, and the quest for it, no matter what form that takes, is always noble.

Kelly: "All I can say is things are changing, but we don't know who's telling the truth and who's not."

I know Kelly's telling the truth. He does it often. He just did it again.

We talked a little about aliens (They're here.), and a little about Bob Marley. (Was he assassinated? Yep. The CIA agent who did it admitted it on his deathbed. Killing terrorists, serial killers, even foreign heads of state, makes some sense, but killing inspirational musicians who just want to make the world a better place? That's just wrong.)

...

ORIGAMI SHALL SET YOU FREE

OK, I'm not going to do this one justice on the page. We're going to need some diagrams. This conspiracy theory is one of the coolest ones I've ever seen. Fold 5, 10 and 20 dollar bills into the same shape, where they're upside down and point like an arrow. They appear to represent one of the Twin Towers at various stages of being on fire. The 5 dollar bill shows a tower, the 10 dollar bill a tower slightly ablaze, and the 20 shows a tower definitively on fire.

I'm not going to go into the standard 9/11 conspiracies here, and there are many, for good reason since that event, too, was clearly at least half-inside job, but this currency hint idea does seem like an admission of some kind, or at least says that America has some very playful, very creative, very bored currency designers.

TOPIC #27: NOTHING COHERENT ENOUGH TO PROPERLY GIVE THIS ONE A TITLE

This was our first meeting in almost a month. Things got busy for a while there. In this last month, what happened?

The election happened. Trump lost. Biden won. Trump whined. Biden tried not to look smug. Trump whined some more. Biden pretended he didn't have early-stage dementia. Democrats celebrated, but in kind of an unfocused way. My brother and I made a bet as to whether Trump would run for president again in 2024 (For the record, he said yes, I said no. His reasoning was that the man couldn't possibly resist the ego strokes of having thousands worship him at his rallies. My thought was that his ego wouldn't allow him to run again, lest he lose. I mean, shit, he's already claiming the election was rigged, even after losing nearly 20 court cases about the outcome of the most heavily-monitored American election ever. He even pre-claimed the election he won was rigged. Ego? Truth? Both? Hard to tell.) The "pandemic" continued. More people in the city wore masks. More people in the country didn't.

This day's discussion was all over the place, so I'll just break it down and summarize. Some days are like this.

...

ELECTION/BUSINESS

Kelly: "Trump knows he lost. Everybody knows."

Me: "I don't know. I think he really is as delusional as he seems, and he lives inside a news bubble where they routinely call him 'The Chosen One.' How could 'The Chosen One' lose in an election to a simple-minded geriatric? It's just not possible."

Kelly: "He knows. Now I'm worried about small businesses."

Me: "You and me both."

Kelly: "I'm just really grateful to my regulars. It's been pretty steady here at the Five Points location. People have been supportive."

We talked a little more about our fears of what the continued pandemic and possible lockdowns (which I don't think are coming, but he's not sure), and how they might affect small business.

...

MASKS

Kelly: "Most people are wearing masks now. People standing outside in line are wearing masks. They're all looking at it one way and not the other way."

Me: "You're back on the immune system thing?"

Kelly: "I never left it."

Me: "And the 'vaccine'?"

Kelly: "I don't trust it. They could be micro-chipping everyone."

Me: "Maybe, but they don't need to. They can already track us anywhere. Traffic cameras, and everyone has one of those stupid beeping rectangles in their pockets. [PAUSE] So, what's the solution?"

Kelly: "We all have to go old-school."

Me: "Like the Amish?"

Kelly: "Exactly."

...

BREAKAWAY COMMUNITIES/JAMAICAN MAROONS

The mention of the Amish, a group of people both of us can't help but respect, lead the discussion into the territory of other breakaway communities, specifically Jamaican Maroon communities. "Maroon" was, and still kind of is, the word for groups of former slaves who ran away from ondage and formed their own societies. In Jamaica the descendants of these Maroon communities are isolated up in the mountains and have remained mostly unfazed by what has since happened in the rest of the world.

Kelly: "Look at a map of Jamaica. Most of the big cities are on the coasts. The inland is mountains. I've been up there before. It's just different. They have their own government. They live their own way. They don't pay nothing to the government. They have their own law."

Me: "Is that where we're all heading? Little individual isolated societies?"

Kelly: "Maybe. It looks like it might be going that way."

...

FEAR

Kelly: "Fear will kill you if you don't pay attention to it."

Me: "We have nothing to fear but fear itself. I may have stolen that line."

...

KAMALA HARRIS

Our new vice-president-elect has Jamaican roots. Kelly is a little miffed that she didn't say anything about her island heritage during the campaign.

TOPIC #28: AGING, ANWAR SADAT, WALMART AND SNAKES

Once again, the conversation was far too unfocused, free range and all-over-the-place for me to summarize it with a neat title that would make any sense. As you've likely noticed by now, when this happens, I just make lists of the topics. The whole point of writing this book (other than having a good excuse to hang out with Kelly) was to focus on the twin ideas of philosophy and fun.

In order for this one to make sense, you're going to need a little background, a mild set-up. I'm a writer and publisher. I run a small, local publishing company named Bilbo Books, which I started with an uber-intellectual arts supporter who was essentially the Crazy Uncle I never had. His name was Bill Bray, but I was introduced to him by his hometown nickname of "Roddy," and you can't just change your name when people have called you the same thing for decades. It didn't work for Prince either. [[Roddy has since passed away. It's as if I've lost my anchor to the world of ideas. I miss you, brother, but I will forever cherish everything you taught me, especially since so much of it is coming true. You were wrong about doctors, though.]]

Anyway, a few months ago, Roddy, who is, at the time of this writing, 83 years old, fell in his apartment and broke his hip. Since then he's been in two hospitals, one rehab facility, had his once bony hip replaced with a metallic one, has had to slow down a little in life (against his better instincts and mostly against his will). Roddy came with me to this meeting, and while he and Kelly were catching up, they talked about aging.

Kelly:"I feel like that sometimes. My dad fell and broke his hip when he was 85, 86, something like that. They couldn't do nothing at the time. It's in the back of my mind now a lot, too. We think we can do anything. At the restaurants I'm always trying to pick up 60, 70 pound boxes, and I don't even have to. I've got people to do stuff like that for me, but I never think of that at the time."

[[[Incidentally, my mentor and eternal friend, Roddy, clearly died from the "vaccine," which they are saying is "perfectly safe," in history's strangest attempt ever at getting people to disbelieve their own eyes. He was on a slow downturn, physically, anyway, I will admit, but the fact that he was "vaccinated" and then got quickly much worse and died within a month is as close to anything I've ever seen at proving the new adage, "The proof is in the poison." Fuck you, Dr. Fauci.]]]

...

THE MARRIAGE OF SUPERSTITION (AND/OR ANCIENT WISDOM) AND BUSINESS
Kelly: "My dad always said, 'If you start a new business on January 1st, it'll keep going all year long.'"

We veer into business discussions a lot. I never knew about the January 1st thing, but I like it. There's something magical about newness: new years, new ideas, new horizons. Kelly went on to give advice about not starting businesses doing things you don't already understand, know and love, and how often you, as the owner, will have to do pretty much every task in the business, at some point, since employees are inevitably not going to show up sometimes. If you can't fill in for them, who will?

This part of that day's talk continued for another 30 minutes or so, but we've covered a lot of it already earlier in this book and in *True Believer*, so I'll fast-forward.

...

AMERICA

Kelly: "America is all right, but this place will kill you."

First off, isn't that an absolutely perfect line? Doesn't that summarize this country in a way that few other sentences could?

Kelly: "In America you work hard. Then you work hard. Then you just die."

Damn, he did it again.

Kelly: "Sometimes I just want to go home and soak my knees in the ocean."

Since Roddy was here, the topic at our table that afternoon was the ways that America has changed in the last fifty years.

Kelly: "America's changed a lot. Some good, some bad. I'm prepared for anything. There are more black folks with more power now. It's a lot freer than it used to be. Racism's still pretty strong, but not as much. On the other hand, everything's so much more expensive now."

Roddy: "In the 60's, my favorite era, there was so much possibility, so much under-the-surface tension. Everything felt like it might implode at any moment, but in an exciting way."

It's hard to argue with any of that. Roddy was a college professor during the Vietnam War, and not only did he once single-handedly stop a riot-in-the-making between pro-war townies and anti-war student "radicals," but he helped plenty of kids stay in school in order to avoid the draft. Hell, I think he even literally hid a few kids from the draft board. In my book, this makes him a hero. War is pretty dumb, especially that one. Kelly, Roddy and I all agree totally that America needs to stop getting involved in other countries' civil wars. Nothing good

ever comes out of that for anyone who doesn't own a weapons factory.
"PANDEMIC"

It's still raging, or at least still around, depending on your point of
view. There is a "vaccine" that has just arrived, two of them as far as
I've heard. Although neither of them fits the definition of a "vaccine"
and are undoubtedly harmful, people still are happy about this, because
so few people have critical thinking skills these days. [[It turns out the
"vaccine" pre-dates the "pandemic." If that isn't proof that it's all a
scam, I don't know what is.]] We talked about propaganda, sickness,
carbon recycling (Kelly always comes back to that one.), how long
people can stand being locked in their houses, how epidemics are monetary opportunities for rich people and just another annoying hassle
for the rest of us. We've covered most of this and will probably do so
again, so let's fast-forward once more.

...

ANWAR SADAT

I have no clue how we got on to the topic of former Egyptian
leader Anwar Sadat, but he is one of the people Kelly admires most
from history. I can't disagree, though Sadat wouldn't be my first go-to
historical hero choice. I'd go with Benjamin Franklin. Writer, wit,
publisher, never afraid of anything, inventor, our first postmaster,
revolutionary who helped foment a rebellion immediately after return-
ing from a gig as British Colonial Ambassador in London, plus a man
who never let war, nor convention, not even marriage get in the way of
having a good time. He even once wrote an essay about why it's better
to hit on older women. It's a good read, still relevant and good advice,
timeless. How can you not love a guy like that?

Kelly: "When he knew he was going to be assassinated, Sadat went
home and changed into his military uniform."

Me: "Hold on. You're saying he changed clothes so he'd be pic-
ture-ready for the casket at his own funeral that he knew was coming?"

Kelly: "Yeah. He was brave enough to face death, but dignified enough to want to look good doing it."

Me: "Wait, you're religious. Isn't pride one the Seven Deadly Sins?"

Kelly: "Yeah, but people still appreciate guys who make a little effort."

JAMAICA

I can pinpoint why our conversation went in this direction. Kelly had mentioned Jamaica earlier, specifically the beautiful and heart-warming imagery of soaking his weary knees in the bright blue waters of the Caribbean. Also,

Kelly: "We still have a Governor General."
Me: "Holdover from colonial days?"
Kelly: "Yeah."

We talked a little about the lingering repercussions of colonialism, about parallels between Jamaica and Canada, about political corruption, habits that are hard to shake, compliance, greed and democracy.

Kelly: "Before the current prime minister took over, the last guy was really corrupt. The current PM, Olness, he's selling out the country as fast as he can."

Sounds vaguely familiar.

WALMART AND THE DEATH OF GREAT MEN

OK, this was pretty cool. When the discussion (somehow) turned to Walmart, and Roddy brought up the name of the founder of that ubiquitous everything store, Sam Walton, Kelly and I both said exactly the same phrase at exactly the same time. How often does that happen outside of Hollywood?

Kelly and Me (in unison): "Sam Walton was a bad-ass."

For real. He was. Sure, today's Walmart isn't what it once was, but as usual, that can be laid at the feet of the founders' decidedly-less-than-bad-ass-unnecessary-sell-out children. Sam Walton sold exclusively American-made products. It was his kids who did a 180 on that, and that's how half our stuff is now made in China. Freaking greedy trust-fund ingrates!

Kelly and I both admire self-made men. Most people do.

SNAKES

Kelly: "Have you ever noticed how there's a snake on that little medicine symbol?"

Me: "The caduceus. Ancient Greek symbol? Snake wrapped around a staff? That one?"

Kelly: "Yeah, but do you know why it's a snake?"

Me: "I honestly don't."

Kelly: "It's all home remedy stuff like my grandmother taught me. Snakes can kill you, but their venom can also cure you. Back in the day they knew this, and that's why there's a snake on the medicine symbol."

Me: "I'll take snake venom over this 'vaccine' any day."

Kelly: "At least snakes don't want to kill you. You're too big to eat."

...

And those were pretty much the highlights of the day's discussion. We also made some bad jokes, talked a little more about medicine, talked a lot more about politics and made some vague plans for the future (all of which weren't interesting enough to be book-worthy).

TOPIC #29: A WHOLE LOTTA TOPICS, ALL REVOLVING AROUND DONALD J. TRUMP

This was our first conversation since the January 6th Washington, D.C., Trump-inspired, election-protesting Capitol Riot, where upper-middle class rednecks and angry soccer moms literally invaded the U.S. Capitol building, looking to murder congress and overturn an election. In fact, Trump's second impeachment conviction Senate trial was on the TV in the background this day, while we free-ranged talked about everything under the sun. I kept waiting for the conversation to go there. To go to the impeachment. It did, but first, once again, it ranged far and wide.

Kelly: "I got inspired to write *True Believer* from starting a business from scratch, then seeing how it grew."

I co-wrote it with him, so I knew that, but both of us run small businesses and small businesses are shutting their doors right and left at the moment, so this is in the backs of all small business owners' minds right now. Kelly dipped into the familiar territory of "putting God first" in all facets of his life, a recurring topic for him – and I would've let it wash over me, but he elaborated.

"One of my friends, Opal, who lives in Florida, called me a couple of days ago, to tell me she overcame lung cancer. I'd been talking to her for years, decades, telling her to put God first, and she finally woke up to what I'd been telling her for decades. It just sort of clicked for her. She started truly treating her body as a temple, like the Bible says, and it cured her cancer."

A DECENT TRUMP ANALOGY

With the Senate trial on in the background, Kelly laid out his basis for hating Trump.

"It's all about disrespect. He disrespected a whole bunch of different groups of people."

Then he segued into Nebuchadnezzar, from the Book of Daniel.

"Daniel warned him that God had given him his power, but Nebuchadnezzar thought he WAS God. Nebuchadnezzar continued to disrespect God, and Daniel warned him again. Daniel said that if he didn't change his ways he was going to wind up losing half his kingdom, and be down on the ground, eating grass like an animal. That's the Trump problem."

It's really hard to argue with that one. Trump has put his own name up in lights, in gold (well, gold-plated, because he's a cheap son of a bitch), in the air. The man creates false idols everywhere he goes. Having a bunch of people telling him that he's God's Gift to America didn't exactly help his Deity Complex.

Kelly's more bullish on Joe Biden than I am. OK, that's not entirely true. As a man, I like Joe Biden, and I'm skeptically hopeful that Joe Biden will bring the country together, but power politics has a way of destroying even the best of intentions. Also, I worry that identity politics and bringing the country together are entirely incompatible and are both being pushed really hard right now. Furthermore, I'm anxious about the side of the two-sided bullshit coin that's been salivating for want of power for the last four years overreaching – because power begets power, which begets nonsense. Just my two cents. [[After not too long in office, it became painfully clear that our Forty-sixth president,

Joseph R. Biden, wasn't even trying to bring the country together, just pushing his own political agenda. Too bad, that man once had the skill set to at least try to bridge our ever-widening partisan gap, but instead he insulted not only rival politicians, but Americans who didn't vote for him, and that never goes down well.]]

Kelly: "Biden's been around. He knows the ropes. But I'll wait and see what happens after his first 100 days in office."

...

RANDOM CONVERSATIONAL TOPIC QUICK SEGUES

We also, briefly, discussed whooping cough, the healing power of garlic, ginger, Vitamin C and Jamaican rum, the unexpected but should've-been-predicted-even-if-only-by-virtue-of-its-being-some-what-inevitable-because-this-is-America fact that, for the first time in years, Kelly ate a fucking hot dog last week, religion, politics, and all the usual stuff.

"Yeah, I ate a hot dog last week. I try to mainly eat fruits and vege-tables, but sometimes you just crave a burger, ya know?"

"Yeah, but a hot dog? Hot dogs are rat anus and chicken beaks…if you're lucky."

"Shut up. I wanted a hot dog. I ate a hot dog."

And I did, indeed, shut up.

...

THAT LITTLE VOICE

If you read *True Believer* you will know about THAT LITTLE VOICE, aka Intuition, aka the message of the gods, aka the thing that guides Kelly's every little step. If you haven't read *True Believer*, then I can't help you. Go and buy that freaking book. It's cheap. It's avail-able at Kelly's restaurants, or, if you must, on those sad, ridiculous, 1984ish online outfits, the most famous of which is named after a river that actually helps the world, unlike its pale corporate counterpart.

Kelly: "I'm still listening. It told me not to wear the mask. It told me to move to a new house. It's told me where to move every time I've moved since the mid-70's. And it's still talking. I'm still listening."

TOPIC #30: OH, INCEDENTALLY, WE BOTH ALSO HATE THAT GENOCIDAL LLAMA-RAPIST, ANTHONY FAUCI

I don't want to imply that either Kelly or I in any way trust America's Trump-foil, Dr. Anthony Fauci, the head of the NIAID (medical advisory board), America's highest-paid professional propagandist, and the man who inspires the widest range of American opinions since Abraham Lincoln. Kelly and I both think he's an evil, lying, sadistic, cardboard, manipulative, lying fascist wearing the disguise of your favorite economics professor…which only makes him more evil. If he looked evil, everyone would recognize he was evil. That's why evil goes out of its way to dress up like goodness.

We didn't have one discussion expressly to discuss this particular shared hatred, but it has cropped up a few times in the course of this pandemic, so I thought I should mention it.

Fauci already had a trial run at his shining evil moment in the sun. In the 1980's he presided over a smaller, more targeted, genocide against gay dudes. If you're old enough to remember (and you'd better be, because this warm-up genocide, this baby step into the exciting world of mass murder, was scrubbed from the internet years ago), this was the guy who promoted giving HIV patients AZT, which even he said would kill them. How that squares with "Do no harm" is beyond me.

Since the original title of novel coronavirus wasn't scary enough, Fauci and his fellow genocidal "health care professionals" renamed it COVID-19, which is, admittedly, scarier sounding and isn't listed on

the backs of Lysol bottles at all.
    Fuck that guy.

TOPIC #31: WE'RE ALL CONNECTED UNDER THE SURFACE, WEED IS GOOD AND WE MAY, SERIOUSLY, BE LIVING OUT "THE BOOK OF REVELATION" RIGHT NOW

"Emancipate yourself from mental slavery"

How's that for a seemingly random mish-mash of chapter discussion topics? Even for a free-flowing conversational duo like the two of us, this day felt a little random. It felt like someone pressed the "Shuffle" button on our souls, sat back and let it play. It was around 3:30 P.M. on a Thursday in June of 2021, the heat of the raging Georgia summer recently dampened a little by daily rains, strangely somewhat tropical in nature, which felt appropriate.

If you're going to catch a restaurant owner when he's not busy, the best time is a weekday afternoon. Mondays and Tuesdays are the safest bets. We humans like to break up our meal routines on our weekends, but weekday restaurant meal rushes are highly predictable. Though he's a pretty laid-back guy, and he likes to play it even more laid-back, Kelly presses the hard work button when he needs to, which is often. Restaurants require routine, daily periods of intense work. Before opening things are busy. During meals, things are busy. On the weekend, forget about it. I don't even try to talk to Kelly on weekends. I learned that lesson one book ago.

I won't try to link today's topics. Surely they were linked, and we did cycle onto some of our greatest hits, but we did an acoustic set today, if I may extend a terrible musical analogy, so they may be familiar tunes, but they sounded like different songs altogether.

EVERYTHING IS ONLY ONE THING

It sounds a little hippie for Kelly. Don't get me wrong, he and I both have some wildly hopeful wishes and hippieish philosophical underpinnings, but as a Jamaican dude being laid back (or in his case appearing laid back) is pretty much expected from him and, while I find that my opinions are constantly changing a little bit each day, the basic idea that we can all get along, love each other, have a lot more sex (preferably in public and hopefully with me), and that we are all somehow entangled together in one large convoluted-but-connected mass, all small parts of one large being feels like it just might be true in my outlook, too.

But when Kelly off-handedly said, "You know, Bo, sometimes I'll be thinking of someone, and they call right then. In that exact moment. It happens a lot," I found it a little alarming coming from him, though I probably shouldn't have. We're both hippies, just fully-employed, semi-useful ones.

You see, I've noticed this phenomenon recently a good bit, too. So, either I'm telepathic or we're all a lot more connected than most people think. While this doesn't bode well for my future career as an X-Man, it's probably the latter. And it makes sense, doesn't it? When you really dig deep into any ecosystem, it's all more intertwined than you thought at first. Big trees are sort of the city planners of the forest. Their roots lay out the avenues for all kinds of underground mini-societies. Have you ever noticed how your dog can spot another dog from miles away, even if there's a marching band, a pile of used diapers and a skyscraper in between them? Dogs know they're connected to other dogs, and they don't care about any of the people who don't feed or play with them. Dogs know it. We think we're far superior to dogs, but we're apparently less observant than schnauzers, and that doesn't even bother us. We really ARE all connected somehow. We just rarely notice. I blame cell phones.

I always blame cell phones, granted, but they are, totally ironically, distancing us from each other all over the world right now. Even you. You think you're immune, but you're not. You're addicted to your telephone. You're so addicted to it that you carry it with you everywhere you go, like a drug, you accessorize it, like a container for drugs, and it's the first thing you want to see in the morning and the last thing you want to see at night, much like, oh what's the word, drugs.

Yes, I know I'm repeating myself from the expressly anti-cell phone chapter, but it's something I believe in so powerfully that it bears repeating.

I ranted about cell phones again, but there is a purpose this time. If we humans are truly so intrinsically connected that we can make someone halfway around the world think of and contact us with literally only their brain, then we're all part of this spinning ball of stardust, all flakes making up the same snowball. But the very device we think connects us does the exact opposite. We don't even need the device, because we're already connected. My basic conclusion is that we're incredibly self-defeating, but capable of giant, pulsating, shining miracles, if only we'd stop texting long enough to recognize it.

...

Kelly went on to talk religion for a bit, but he lost me somewhere around accusing preachers of just regurgitating stuff they learned in seminary instead of actually teaching anything to their congregations. I think there's a higher power, a god, but I don't know the details, and I'm not sure we're supposed to. Kelly has more definite ideals, but I doubt seriously if he's crossed the threshold of a church in this century. Yes, he knows the Bible inside and out, but he's not a church-goer, so I'm not sure I should listen to his take on what's happening in church.

I did, however, perk right back up and jolt to attention once again when he turned the conversation toward how awesome he and I are.

Kelly: "You and I move freely. Almost nobody else does, but we do. We have free minds, free consciousnesses, free thought."

Me: "Indeed we are vastly superior to everyone else. I couldn't agree more."

Kelly: "No, for real, we're free. There are some other free people around, even here, but not many."

Me: "Fear. Fear and cell phones. I think, down deep, most people want to be free, but they've been sp conditioned to be too afraid to be able to access the free little person inside themselves."

Kelly: "Little person?"

Me: "Yes, we each have an open-minded, optimistic, loving, angelic dwarf inside us, but he gets his ass kicked by the ogres of anger, beaten by the mobs of malice and drowned by the faucet of fear. Damn, Kelly, was that poetic or what?"

No answer.

We spoke a little about evil and I asked him a question I've always meant to ask, but never remembered to before this day.

Me: "Do you think the devil is a real thing? An actual being?"

Kelly: "Yeah. There's good and there's evil. God and Satan."

Me: "OK, I guess I expected you'd say that and all, but it's not as good a discussion topic as I thought it'd be. If there's a devil, is he red? Does he have a tail? Horns? A pitchfork? And if so, why does he need a pitchfork? Is he farming evil corn?"

Kelly, wisely, ignored this one.

...

LIZARD PEOPLE

While talking about evil, we did veer into classic Conspiracy Theory territory. The lizard people. We didn't delve too deeply into the deep end of this one, though if I can remember, I should bring it up at our next talk. I'm pretty sure Kelly thinks that there are lizard people, reptiles wearing human skin, going around doing evil stuff. I'm not sure that there aren't lizard people, but I'm also not convinced that just because a guy is evil that means that he's got scaly skin under his fake human overcoat. He could just legitimately suck as a human being.

...

ARE WE LIVING THE END TIMES OUT RIGHT NOW?

I sure as hell hope not. I've never ridden a swamp boat across the Okefenoke. I've never drunk absinthe on top of Mt. Fuji. I've never even been to Amsterdam, and I should probably do that before the world ends. It'll be less fun post-Apocalypse.

Although The End of Days is a common Kelly topic, and although I'm a lot more skeptical (seeing as this has been predicted millions of times throughout history, and, as far as I can tell, has never actually happened), even I have to begrudgingly admit that there certainly are more Apocalyptic signs now than I've ever seen before. Of course, we did just pull ourselves out of a worldwide pandemic, so it's kind of to be expected, isn't it?

Kelly is pretty sure the COVID-19 Vaccine IS The Mark of the Beast. He may be right. I hope not, but maybe.

Kelly: "Once I heard that Bill Gates had a hand in the 'vaccine,' I knew it was really the Mark of the Beast. He's been saying the world is overpopulated for years."

Me: "I guess he is one of the few people rich and powerful enough to actually get away with killing off a few million people in the name of charity without anyone noticing. Plus his hair has always looked pretty evil to me. He's like a satanic Moe from 'The Three Stooges.'"

Kelly: "It's the Mark of the Beast, Bo. If we don't have our minds geared up for it, we're going down, too. If they don't convince enough people to get the vaccine, they'll find another way to get it into us."

Me: "I can buy the idea that the world is running out of resources and the population is growing too fast to keep up. Look at world population charts sometime. There was a slow and steady rise for centuries and then the 20th century hits and BAM, there are now six billion more people. It makes sense that we'd be running low on pretty much everything with that many people."

Kelly: "This stuff, this 'vaccine' is liquid. It's like quicksilver, and it goes all over your body."

Me: "OK, I see what you're saying. Like you, I have no problem totally seeing the thought control aspect of this whole corona fear thing. I'm with you on the ending small businesses, corralling critical thinkers, and killing off old people too stubborn and set in their ways to follow the Pied Piper of Doom."

Kelly: "Yes, they want to kill off all of the old people, control the minds of the young people///"

Me (interjecting): "Through the cell phones."

Kelly: "Yep, and the kids really believe what they see on the cell phones, so they're easy to control. Older people know better and can see the whole picture, but once all the old people get their Mark of the Beast, they can be killed off at any time, and then all that's left are the guys on top and a bunch of sheep down below."

Me: "Yeah, no doubt about the mind control. Now that I think of it, we modern people, with our democracy and our dog sweaters and our techno-bullshit, we think our world is totally different than it was back in the Middle Ages, but with a tiny fraction of people owning everything, controlling the rest of us and rigging the system in their favor, it doesn't seem at all different than feudalism. We're the serfs, we just don't know it anymore."

Even though I love this stuff, it was feeling a bit too heavy for me at that moment, so I scanned the area for a change of subject. Looking out Kelly's front window, I couldn't help but notice that the city had put up an anti-marijuana billboard right outside the town's premier Jamaican Restaurant. That can't be coincidence. It read, "85% of your peers don't smoke marijuana," which, of course, is a complete and utter lie. Total crap. I pointed the propaganda-in-the-sky out to him.

Kelly: "Yeah, they're afraid because herb opens up consciousness and makes people less violent."

Me: "And they need us to keep killing each other to maintain control. Also, they don't want stoned soldiers. Nobody wants stoned soldiers."

Kelly: "In the 70's America even tried to wipe out Jamaica's herb. They flew crop-dusters and dropped stuff to kill the plants over the fields. But it didn't work. Three weeks later, the herb just grew back."

Me: "What I don't get is how weed's so legal in Oregon that there are above-board weed stores and weed delivery services, and you can legitimately put Pot Dealer on your resume in Portland, but you can still get arrested for it in Mississippi. With all the money that can be made off it, even some hard-core Republicans are making getting into it. Former Republican Speaker of the House John Boehner, not the coolest guy around, is now a weed dealer. But you can still lock up black kids in Texas for carrying around a small baggie full of a native plant? Insanity, Kelly, total insanity."

Kelly: "Good things always migrate East from the West. Look at the Sixties."

Me: "Damn, now I wish I'd been born twenty years earlier. I just missed the Sixties, and had to grow up in the 80's. We had synthesizer music, but no free love. I'd trade all three 'Back to the Future' movies for having sex with hippie chicks in a public park any day."

And that seemed like a good place to end that day's discussion.

TOPIC #32: THE END OF THE WORLD
or
JUST THE END OF THE WORLD AS WE KNOW IT?

Arriving at Kelly's second restaurant this day, I had no idea I would receive
a sign that it's either the end of the world…or even just the end of
this book. I knew Kelly had a regular who was an official End Times
prophet, an Apocalyptic predictioneer who kind of wanted the world
to end. I've heard Kelly talk about the guy, but I never thought I'd
meet him. The Apocalyptic preacher is almost an archetype, it's that
common, all over the world, but here The Bible Belt we've always had
more than our fair share.

This one's name is Richard Perry. Tall, shaved head, politely im-
posing, a thoroughly knowledgeable zealot, and just a wee bit crazy.
What I'll never understand is why these guys want the world to end. It
seems wildly sadistic. Even if he's right about all of it, it's not a nice
thing to wish for.

This guy takes End Times prophesying to new heights. Not only
does he know The Book of Revelation and other popular End Times
texts inside and out, but the dude's got the end of the world all mapped
out, with dates, maps, color-codes, a full on End of Days workbook.
Apparently, according to Richardamus, the world began to end on
September 11th (when The First Seal was broken). We're in a period
of wars and rumors of wars, which is, of course, true, but then again
hasn't that always been true? The Antichrist will be among us soon

enough.

Oh, and Richard's got an exact date. That's helpful.

There will be a War with Iran, or rather a war that starts in Iran and spreads and spreads, eventually becoming World War III. And then all the comic book stuff will happen: lakes of fire, dragons, virgins, the Antichrist, The Rapture, etc.

On the off-chance that this crazy Apocalyptic preacher guy is actually right, it's worth at least buying his book, if not taking up the habit of giving out caviar and toast points to homeless dudes. I don't know, Richard may be right. I doubt it. I really hope not. But you never know. It's pretty hard to argue with the idea that there's a lot of crazy shit happening in the world right now.

But the world's always been crazy. It's just that people now have 24/7 news in our pockets (except for Kelly and me), and since, even if you mistakenly think it's real, the "news" is actually just the "bad news," I can see how it might seem like the world will come to an end in the 2030's.

Richard Perry has it all mapped out. If he weren't talking about THE END OF THE WORLD, it would just be kind of impressive and interesting.

Richard believes what he says. Kelly believes a lot of it, but is hazier on the details, including the exact date, and I'm extremely skeptical.

Either way, this chance meeting (Or was it?) may not have shown me the End of the World, but it definitely prophesied the End of this Book. For a philosophical book about fear, control, manipulation, hope, love and ox tail, ending the story with a rousing, cocksure conversation with a Doomsday Prophet feels right.

A bit of advice – When talking to a zealot, don't expect a free-flowing, two-way conversation. Those guys are good talkers, but not such good listeners.

In case you don't have a crazy uncle, here are the highlights of the End of Days:

The Unbelievers and The Disobedient are pretty screwed. They shalt be wipethed from the face of the Earth. I don't know exactly what that meanseth, but it doth not soundeth particularly goodeth.

The Believers (presumably also The Obedient) will be Raptured with their flesh and blood. This was news to me, the flesh and blood part. Remind me again why we need spleens, noses and rectums in the Afterlife? I don't know how Afterlife Taco Bell, clouds and gravity factor in here, but I suppose it's better than being wiped out.

Taking the Lord's name in vain is a much bigger deal than I thought. I thought it was just a few cuss words, but apparently it's more of a way of life. I liked this passionate assertion of Richard's. It makes sense. Also, it gets you off-the-hook for a few off-hand god-damns when you drop a brick on your toes.

Metaphor and literalism are more intertwined than I thought. I'm of the school that believes that holy texts are great metaphorical works of art. Kelly is a humble literalist. Richard is so sure he's right that he can distinguish between what's literal and what isn't. I really hope Richard's not right.

You should read one of Richard's books. Kelly and I will give you a list in an appendix. Even if you think the guy's totally wrong, they're interesting. I think he's 180 degrees, full on hokey-pokey wrong, and yet I've found the two I've read utterly fascinating.

...

Since I don't have the patience to keep writing this book until the world sees through the massive corona-lies and turns this Orwellian nonsense around, and since Kelly has a little Apocalypse in him, too, and since we've all thought about the end of the world at least a few times in the last few years, and since the Powers That Be are now channeling their inner Antichrist and predicting less-than-Rapturous death for us all (unless of course we let them poison us and our children with their fake vaccines "fakeccines?"), talking to an End Times preacher who's a Kelly's regular feels like an absolutely perfect way to end this book.

...

The world will not end.

Hope will not end.

Even though it looks dire for free-thinkers at the moment, we shall prevail.

Unlike the Powers That Be, many of us free-thinkers actually like other people.

Kelly doesn't just like people. You might even say he loves them.

...

And, as always, the way to beat back lies, manipulation, power grabs, fake news, and the endless stream of fear-mongering flowing from the petty billionaires, pharma genocideistas, and authoritarian types, Woke mafia types, and to inspire the far-too-fearful masses and spin their heads around and around (metaphorically) until they stop believing what they're being spoon-fed, until they're finally, at long last, able to question everything, to live without fear, to boldly strut into the future with their heads held high and generosity in their hearts starts with the simplest act of them all. The solution to all of the bullshit is what John Lennon, Jesus Christ, and Bob Marley preached – LOVE.

Love conquers all.

Love laughs at fear.

Love steps neatly over manipulation and hurdles propaganda.

Love connects us, inflates our goodness, swallows our fear and hatred, and launches us through the stratosphere and into the cosmic reality of The Age of Enlightenment, The Age of Wonder, The Age of Aquarius. This is the dawning of that amazing age. All we need to do is smile at the fear, laugh at the lies, hold each other tight and take off in a dead sprint toward a better tomorrow. Kelly and I will save you a seat.

...

THE END (of the book, not the world)

EPILOGUE

Kelly and I would like to issue a warning to our readers which may help them avoid the trap that *Dune* author, Frank Herbert, warned us about when he wrote that "Fear is the mind killer."

1) **Cut waaaaaaayyyyyy back on the time you spend online.** We recommend smashing your cell phone, but if you're not going to do that, at least learn to limit yourself.

2) **If you follow warning #1, take your copious new free time, tilt your head upward and look around.** You're living in a beautiful world, with beautiful people, beautiful ideas, a world full of more possibilities than ever before. Take advantage of this scenario.

3) **Do something good every day.**

4) **Make fun of someone bad every day.**

5) **Don't take yourself so damn seriously.** Have you looked at yourself in the mirror lately? Trust me, there's humor there. You're an idiot. Don't' worry, I am, too. We all are. And that's okay.

6) **Question everything you're being told.** You don't need to be obnoxious about it, but you really shouldn't swallow anything you're being told without at least doing a little research of your own. Those who are telling you what "reality" is probably have an agenda. Once you look into it a little, it all gets clearer. And it doesn't even take that much research to arrive at this obvious conclusion. They don't hide their motives as well as they think.

7) Try a little philosophizing yourself.

8) Have fun.

Philosophy and fun. Not a bad combination, if Kelly and I do say so ourselves.

ADDENDA

You may have noticed a few grammatical inconsistencies, and, since I'm a publisher, I feel the need to explain. While both Kelly and I believe that this virus was entirely overblown, completely manmade, and obviously a planned event to facilitate the theft of our privacy and money, it was still an actual disease. If you were very old, very fat or had a pre-existing lung condition, it was serious. It did kill a number of people who fit one or more of those categories, and America has more than our share of all three categories, especially the fat one. So, while both Kelly and I saw through the lies, I'd still like to acknowledge that it was, to a degree, real, and world-wide, so I vacillated on putting the quotation marks, with their implied sarcasm, around the word "pandemic" every time. There, I hedged enough not to be totally insulting to those who really did lose loved ones. And, since I even want to hedge on this explanation, and ensure that I'm NOT, in any way, apologizing to the multitudes who didn't lose loved ones, but felt that their virtue-signaling nonsense gave them license to put down those of us who were free-thinking enough to see through the governmental lies, those without the discernment God gave most of our more intelligent porpoises, to you I say "Fuck off, wake up and start watching the news with a degree of critical thinking. Stop thinking you're smarter than the rednecks. Those guys saw through this nonsense right away. Thank you, rednecks, for laying down the yellow bricks and skeptical mortar on the beautiful road to Enlightenment."

...

RANDOM:

"Politics really IS like a horse race. I used to go to the track a lot, and I knew how to bet on horses. I know horses. The one who jumps out to the early lead never wins the race. Winners start slow, save their energy and then break out to win the race. It's the same way with politics." – Kelbourne "Kelly" Codling

"I'm so amazed to see so much of what I predicted would happen, happening." – also Kelly

...

JAMAICAN HOLIDAYS (in case you were curious or wanted a good excuse to party):

Labor Day – May 23rd
Emancipation Day – August 1st
Independence Day – August 6th

Bob Marley's Birthday – February 6th (He is, understandably, a national hero, and we like celebrating birthdays of national heroes, especially those who were murdered and those who left a wildly hopeful legacy we can dance to.)

BIBLIOGRAPHY

...

Codling, Kelbourne and Craig, Bowen, *True Believer*, Bilbo Books Publishing, Athens, Georgia, 2018.

Perry, Richard H., *The Time Has Come: Our Journey Begins*, self-published, printed in Columbia, SC, 2011.

Toffler, Alvin, *Future Shock*, Bantam Books, 1984.